YOUR
new
NOW

Other Helpful, Inspiring Books
from Nicki Koziarz

5 Habits of a Woman Who Doesn't Quit

A Woman Who Doesn't Quit Bible Study

*Why Her? 6 Truths We Need to Hear When Measuring Up
Leaves Us Falling Behind*

*Rachel & Leah Bible Study: What Two Sisters Teach Us
about Combating Comparison*

*Flooded: The 5 Best Decisions to Make When Life Is Hard
and Doubt Is Rising*

*Flooded Study Guide: The 5 Best Decisions to Make
When Life Is Hard and Doubt Is Rising*

YOUR *new* NOW

Finding Strength and Wisdom
When You Feel Stuck Where You Are

NICKI KOZIARZ

BETHANYHOUSE
a division of Baker Publishing Group
Minneapolis, Minnesota

© 2023 by Nicki Koziarz

Published by Bethany House Publishers
Minneapolis, Minnesota
www.bethanyhouse.com

Bethany House Publishers is a division of
Baker Publishing Group, Grand Rapids, Michigan

Printed in the United States of America

ISBN 978-0-7642-3700-3 (paper)
ISBN 978-0-7642-4162-8 (casebound)
ISBN 978-1-4934-4074-0 (ebook)

Library of Congress Cataloging-in-Publication Control Number: 2022044043

Cover design by Alison Fargason

The author is represented by the Brock, Inc. Agency.

Baker Publishing Group publications use paper produced from sustainable forestry practices and post-consumer waste whenever possible.

23 24 25 26 27 28 29   7 6 5 4 3 2 1

"Life is full of transitions. Some are fun. Some are downright frightening. All come with at least a twinge of fear about the unknown path that lies ahead. If you are in a season of wondering, *What's next?* or questioning, *Why now?*, Nicki Koziarz has created a valuable and biblical resource that will help you keep from overthinking the coming changes. Her keen insight and solid Bible teaching will empower you to navigate your current transitions not only with a calm in your heart but with a spring in your step. *Your New Now* will be a clarifying companion to both assure and quiet your heart on your journey to what is next."

Karen Ehman, *New York Times* bestselling author and
coauthor of *Trusting God in All the Things*;
Proverbs 31 Ministries speaker; wife, mom,
and Grandma Kit to baby Jasper

"With four children in high school through college and one almost married, I feel like every few months wear the label and title of this book. Everything that felt so far away years ago comes barreling at me, and it seems like as soon as I settle into *now*, *new* enters the picture again. In *Your New Now*, Nicki Koziarz gives hope to that hard place with practical advice and insight on how to live today for what it is, finding strength in exactly where God has you. This is a much-needed message and a must-read book for every woman feeling stuck in the in-between!"

Ruth Schwenk, coauthor of *Trusting God in All the Things*

"If you have ever asked God, 'What now?' in a changing season of your life, Nicki is the friend you need to walk with you. With biblical truth and grace-filled reliability, Nicki guides you through each step of what it means to trust God through change."

Ashley Morgan Jackson, Christian speaker;
author of *Tired of Trying*

"Often as believers we find ourselves in the middle ground between our promises from God and the fulfillment of them. Nicki gives personal testimonies and a blueprint to assist readers in navigating this space. We believe that every person who reads this book will be impacted greatly by the wisdom and strategies she shares. We highly recommend Nicki and *Your New Now* to every person in those in-between spaces of life."

LaJun and Valora Cole, lead servants of Contagious Church; authors of *Divine Dispatch*

"This book feels like sitting with a cup of tea and an old friend—someone who knows you well and has walked with you through the highs and lows of your life. Each chapter features God's Word, allowing His truth to resonate in your heart and mind amid times of transition. For those who have cried out, wondering if anyone understands the loss and heartbreak you've been through, there is comfort in knowing you are not alone in your questions. Regardless of difficult seasons we may navigate, Nicki's practical responses guide us to choices that create good fruit and reveal the glory of God."

Arielle Gaiser, *Your New Now* focus group participant

"I will never read Moses's story again without seeing the clear transition seasons, thanks to the words in this book. With humor and humility, Nicki perfectly pairs memorable personal stories with powerful Scripture verses from both Old and New Testaments. This is a book that points to the power and presence of God no matter what season you are in!"

Amanda Greenwood, *Your New Now* focus group participant

"We all go through transitions and changing seasons in life, and Nicki brings comfort, truth, and practical steps to navigate these seasons from a biblical perspective. Reading this book was the healing process I needed but didn't know would be so beneficial and impactful on my life! I'm a young adult, and Nicki gave me tools that will be helpful for the rest of my life, no matter what the season."

Brooke Slagle, *Your New Now* focus group participant

To my daughter, Kennedy Grace.
Seasons come and seasons go,
but the Grace of God will always
remain evident in your life.
I'm proud of who you are becoming,
and I can't wait to see the rest of God's story
for your life unfold.

Acknowledgments

To my husband, Kris, and our family, thank you for your love, support, and grace for this writing season. I love all of you more than I knew was possible, and you are all my greatest joy.

Meredith Brock, I know I am so blessed to have you in my corner, and your wisdom, support, and brilliance on this project have been the greatest gift. Thank you for being the best agent possible.

Glynnis Whitwer, I get tears in my eyes when I think about your initial text back to me after I asked for your help with this project. Thank you for saying yes, thank you for helping me be a better communicator and for pushing me as a writer. Your incredible editing work made this book better.

Lysa TerKeurst and the Proverbs 31 Ministries team, I'm grateful to be part of a ministry like this. Thank you, Lysa, for your support and wisdom for me and countless other writers.

David Abernathy, thank you for your wisdom, insight, and theological understanding for this project. I'm so thankful for your guidance and help.

Katie Haines, I couldn't have done this without you. Thank you for your time, support, encouragement, and the ability to put feedback and research data into a spreadsheet faster than anyone I know. Your fingerprints are all over this message, thank you!

Lindsey Smith and Trixie, thank you so much for our study day and your love, prayers, and wisdom! So thankful for the both of you. You helped bring so much clarity to this project!

LaJun and Valora Cole, divine appointments are my favorite. Thank you for your wisdom, awareness of the Holy Spirit, and the way you follow after God!

To the *Your New Now* focus group and Rebecca I., wow. Your wisdom and insight into this book were everything I needed for this process. Thank you!

Bethany House Publishers team, thank you for the opportunity to partner for this book.

Contents

To the Reader

Hi, if we haven't met before, I'm Nicki.

I could start this letter by telling you a bunch of nonsense about the other books and studies I've written and blah, blah, blah. Or, I could tell you a funny story about my past or life on the farm where we live.

But when I pick up a new book, I don't really care about those things.

What I'm wondering when I decide to read something is . . . *Does this author even understand what I'm going through?*

We've all read books by people who seemed to have their lives so perfectly tied up into a bow, we couldn't make it past the first chapter. As I'm typing, my hair hasn't been washed in over four days. I'm wearing the T-shirt I slept in last night (but I did put on a fresh pair of workout leggings, because I still think if I get dressed for the gym, I may actually go). And to top it off, I'm wearing a hat that says, "Farm Fresh." *Classy, classy, y'all.*

This book and this writing is me, full of flaws, frustrations, and fears. And I've been in a space in time where I feel like I've been asking more internal questions about my life than I've found answers for.

Because I was warned.

That life would one day feel like it was passing me by, and I couldn't catch it or slow it down if I tried. And it did. Life transitioned again and again. And multiple times over the last few months, I've found myself asking one main, overarching question: *What am I supposed to do now?*

There are dozens of books out there to help us find purpose and passion. But there aren't a whole lot of people who are talking about what you do in the in-between spaces of life.

It's the space of when you aren't where you were but you're not where you're going yet either . . . *What do we do there?*

This is why this book is titled *Your New Now*. It's not so much about where you've been (although you will look back on your childhood a little), and it's not really about where you're going. It's about what we need to learn in the here and now. It's about finding strength, wisdom, and hope for the current space you find your soul settling into.

The truth is, change in life is the one constant we can count on.

And yes, there are things that can change in an instant. We can go to bed one day with one status and wake up the next with another. But what I've found is that most transitions in life come on slowly.

Researcher and author Bruce Feiler tells us we will go through a significant change every twelve to eighteen months. He also says we will go through three to five major changes in our lifetime that can take four to five years to fully transition through.[1]

Think about all the transitions our bodies and souls go through in a lifetime. None of them are fast. And I am so thankful nineteen-year-old Nicki's soul isn't the same as forty-two-year-old Nicki's soul.

The slow sculpting of our souls is something to be sacredly held.

I've learned some really hard lessons about transitions in life. For example, life's seasons don't always end up looking the way we had hoped. But each time we allow ourselves to grow in the in-between spaces of life, we become wiser, stronger, and then eventually we are ready to head into that next season of our life.

I found someone in the Bible who has a lot to teach us about the in-between spaces of life. His name: Moses.

In this book, I've lined up Moses's life next to what I'm calling the four seasons of transition. We're using the word *season* because, as we just learned, change often takes time. Seldom do we change overnight or learn a lesson in a week. And seasons do eventually end. You will make it through all the changes life brings you.

Moses managed some of his transition seasons really well. And some he didn't. But ultimately Moses was a man who finished well, and that's the greatest lesson transitions can teach us—*how to finish well.*

Fair warning, you may also find yourself in multiple seasons of transition at the same time. We'll talk more about that in the first section of the book.

But before we move on, I'd like to cover some details.

First, I highly recommend reading this book with at least one other person. You will want to process some of what you learn, and come to understand about yourself, with someone else. You can even join an online community to discuss what you learn. Look for a group on Facebook called *Your New Now Conversations.*

Second, if you enjoy studying the Bible, I'm so thrilled to tell you there's a *free* Bible study right here in this book! Between each section you'll find a mini Bible study that goes with the chapters you just read. So read the chapters and then do the study. This will be great for group studies as well!

And lastly, be kind to yourself in this process. This book is filled with a lot of biblical and practical help for your life's transitions. But your process is still your process. Take things slowly. Let God do a deep work in you. And don't be afraid to reach out for some professional help from a licensed counselor if you feel like you need more guidance.

Alright, time to get started, see you in chapter one!

Your friend,
Nicki

DEVELOPMENT

1

The Four Seasons

I swallow the lump in my throat as I begin to type these words.

My heart drops a few notches. And I settle into the place I am... *today*. It's hard for me to recognize and value the space of time I'm currently in. Most days, I'm a woman who is either looking ahead or behind.

But today, I look out the window and see the signs of seasonal change. Dead leaves. Brown grass. Cloudy skies with a cooler breeze. The sun occasionally peeking out.

The date on the calendar and the temperature on my weather app tell me a new season is coming: *fall*.

Summer is my favorite season, and I wish it would linger just a bit longer. Whether I like it or not, *the signs are starting to show change is coming.*

Our dog sits at my feet, snorting while he snores. His face has little white hairs on it where his puppy dun-and-black coat used to be so shiny and bright. I find myself wondering how much time we have left with this little pug.

His puppy days are far behind him. He's sat faithfully by my side for every book I've ever written, and today I look at him and wonder if this will be our last.

He's getting older, and *the signs are starting to show that something is changing.*

I push back my glasses and feel the wrinkle cream left on my face from the night before. My skin is . . . how do they say it? Maturing. And *the signs are starting to show things in my body are changing.*

The house is quiet, for the first time in what seems like years.

The wooden front porch isn't as littered with shoes because my family has finally learned to put them away. The mornings are less chaotic. The calendar isn't filled with birthday parties and sleepovers. The three daughters we raised on this farm for the last eight years are getting older, and *the signs are starting to show that life is changing.*

Time has carried on, and *all the signs are starting to show, change is coming.*

Just as the seasonal signs are showing out the window now, life's changes have been showing for a while. I just didn't quite notice until now.

They said this would happen. That it would all go by so quickly. And it did.

But this quiet space in this season of life won't be this way for long. Because as I'm typing these words, we are preparing to welcome three beautiful boys to our family through adoption. It's a complicated story. Half that is mine, half that isn't. So, I'll share as much as I can throughout this book, but what I need you to know is this is one strange season I'm in.

The coming and going of children in our home. The literal changes and transitions happening inside our house to accommodate three more bodies who need places to sleep. It all feels so strange and somehow so right.

But there's still something inside me wondering if I'm in the right place at the wrong time with the wrong outfit.

Maybe you can understand what this feels like? It's like the season changed from summer to fall and you are still hanging on to your Birkenstock sandals and cut-off jean shorts while everyone else is in Uggs, leggings, and oversized sweatshirts. Some people would say, "Who cares, wear what you want!"

And to a certain extent, I agree, but that's not what this feels like.

It's like a place of denial. You know you *should* wear something warmer, but you refuse, because the season changed and no one, especially not you, gave it permission to change.

The calendar pages keep flipping. Life keeps changing. And one day you look up and it all looks so different than you thought it would.

We plan what we want life to look like.

We create five-year vision plans.

We think we know where it's all headed.

Sometimes change seems so far away, but then boom, it's right in front of us. Life can change really fast, and we feel like we're playing a grown-up version of hide-and-seek . . . *ready or not, here it comes.*

There's the unexpected death of someone we love. The job loss or change. The relationship that we thought would last forever doesn't. The world gets hit by a pandemic. Finances decline. We send the kids to kindergarten. We send the kids to college. A move to a new city tempts us.

And so, we find ourselves in this weird place between what was and what will be. The place we often call *transition.*

Here, uncertainty is certain. The scene is ending, but the rest of the script seems blank. We sense a cliffhanger awaits, but we wonder why the director doesn't step in and direct the next scene.

Sometimes transition is ugly and sometimes it's beautiful. But the fortunate thing is that even what starts ugly has the opportunity to end in beauty. Beauty for ashes. Joy for mourning. Praise for heaviness.

Few of us cry out for help when transition is good. That's easy to celebrate! But there's another side to change, which can come in the hurtful words spoken from others about our change, the aches in our souls of longing for what was, the tears that stem from fear of the future, the feelings of being unseen as we wander into something new. The wondering what to do next, the looking back and asking if things could have been different ... *not so beautiful.* These things and so much more are the real places transition lands our emotions. And I think there's a common question we're all asking.

The "Now What?" Question

Whether the transition we experienced or are experiencing has made us feel trapped or free, many of us still find ourselves asking this question: "OK, now what?"

The "Now what?" question has us looking into a wide-open space that seems to have many options. But really, at this moment, it's not about the path we choose to take. It's more about the reaction to the changing of the season or the pause on the path we are on today.

> When our reaction to transition becomes one of choosing to grow rather than needing to know, we become learners of life's greatest lessons.

I once heard that fear and anger can mess up a human soul more than anything. And every transition we go through has at least one of those two emotions easily tied to it. Probably because every transition in life is the ending of something before it is the beginning of something else. And beginnings and endings can create anxiety.

The highs and lows of life as it flows from season to season are so defining for our souls. This process reveals what is happening deep in those places within us where no one goes except God. When our souls are becoming defined by a transition, whether in a negative or positive aspect, those deep places within us start to overflow with the reflection of what is inside us.

And when it's good, it comes out good. But when it's bad, *whew* . . . it comes out real bad.

Most of the time you can tell what's deep inside someone's soul by the way they react to someone else's transition of life. Are they happy or hopeful for the other person? Probably a good reflection. Or do they have criticism, bitterness, or jealousy? Probably a bad reflection.

Think about the last time someone told you about a change in their life. What was your initial response? If the reflection is messy, we may have some internal work to do.

> Our response to what's happening
> around us brings awareness to what's
> reflecting from within us.

All of this is why there's a lump in my throat today. Because all these emotions, all these feelings, all of these reflections, are very real to me. Some good. Some bad.

What does a girl who just likes to have fun and live life to the fullest in the summer do when the season changes? How do I move from one season to the next and not carry the regret or constant replays from the season before? How do I find peace when I'm not quite ready for the next season?

Maybe you're reading these words and you think you have the perfect advice for me. Or maybe you are reading this and thinking, *Ya, girl… What do we do with all this?*

I'm realizing no one ever talked to me about how to transition well from space to space and season to season. And in some places of transition, I feel like I'm doing this thing great. But in other areas, I feel like I'm failing miserably. Many of you reading this probably feel the same. Like our souls are in some middle ground between what we once knew as "now" and where we're going next.

This middle ground can also become a battleground, because it's the place the enemy of our souls wants us to stay stuck. Because here, on this battleground, we can continue to feel lost, lonely, and lack direction in our lives.

> When your middle ground
> becomes your battleground,
> it's time to fight for your future.

The future can start to look more blurry than bright if we're not careful.

But we cannot just wing it through transition anymore. We need something really practical to get us from here to there with our heads held high… a strategic battle plan. We need to get on this battleground equipped for the battle.

So, what do we do?

Starting Points

A good starting point is to acknowledge change has come or it is coming. And whether it caught us off guard or we expected every second of it, it's here.

It's our new now. The space we are in, *today*.

Second, we learn to accept every emotion and feeling that comes with the transition. And we must recognize emotions to come to acceptance.

Third, we make the decision that we're going to get this sorted out in our souls. We'll sit with this place of change and transition in our lives, surrendering our will and emotions to the Lord, until we can see hope again and we can make sure the secret place, where no one goes but God, is a good place again.

And then, we start to learn every lesson God wants this transition season to teach us. We might need some new skills, habits, or perspectives, and those things will come. We might need a deeper understanding of His Word and a greater awareness of His presence.

The anger and fears may all still be there tomorrow, but for today, we can exhale and take a break for just a minute. Transitions in life don't have to break us, make us gain fifteen pounds of stress weight, or cause us to lose who we were before the transition hit.

Through the help of Moses's story in the Bible, I promise you, we're going to learn to get through these messy places. And whether you're the college girl getting ready to graduate with a degree you feel you have no use for, or the corporate woman who has finished her climb to the top of the ladder, or somewhere else, we need to learn the lessons Moses offers us in his process.

I believe Moses went through more transitions than anyone we could study in the Bible. His story, with God's words, through the Bible, is going to help us. You will find some resolve in your soul about the season you are in and learn to prepare for what's coming next.

And one day, you're going to walk with someone else through their transition. When you do, you'll be able to remind them— they may feel lost today, but they will find their way too.

But first, we're gonna start with you.

1. Write down one place of transition (or more) you are in today:

   _____

2. What emotion do you feel attached to the above transition? Anger? Fear? Or something else?

   _____

Describe what you think the root of these emotions are and then pray and ask the Lord to help you sort through this.

Meeting Moses

Chances are, you have heard of the Bible hero Moses before.

Even if you didn't grow up in the Church or attend a vacation Bible school as a kid, I would guess you had the TV on during Easter and have maybe seen promotions for the replay of the 1956 movie *The Ten Commandments*. That's our guy, Moses.

He has an incredibly fascinating story. And other than Jesus, Moses is the only person whose life is explained in such depth from birth to death in the Bible. This is why we can learn so much about transitions from him.

We can learn about other people's lives from the Bible too, like Jacob or Joseph. But not to the extent that Moses's life is laid out for us.

Here's why this is important.

As we study Moses, I'm going to ask you to study your life.

If you're asking questions like, "Now what?" or "How do I find out what's next?" we may need to look back on some experiences in your life and identify a few reasons why you are in this place of transition.

When we're struggling with something spiritually in life, one of the greatest things we can do is to look at someone in the Bible who can teach us how to not only go through it but also grow through it. That's why this book is filled with examples from the Bible.

The Bible is a story about God. And God hasn't changed since the days of Moses. Through the Bible, we get to study biblical heroes of faith and apply their victories, failures, and wisdom to our own struggles. There is power in that, because God is found in every story through the Scriptures, and every story in the Bible points to Jesus.

> **Jesus is the only true and long-lasting answer to our soul's deepest struggles.**

Moses is someone I can relate to, and I have a feeling you might too. If you've ever failed, doubted yourself, flat-out disobeyed God, or felt like you had something that disqualified you in life (if I had four hands they'd all be raised right now), then you will see how his story will challenge the way you see yours.

Moses found himself in quite a few places where he asked the "Now what?" questions of life. Sometimes his *new now* happened slowly, but other times his life changed quickly.

We first meet Moses in Exodus 2, when he is about to enter into the first major transition of his life: from birth to adoption. Though his life account begins in the book of Exodus, we see his name mentioned throughout the Old and New Testament books of the Bible.

The book of Exodus is the second book of the Bible, and a lot has happened when we arrive in Exodus 2. A wide variety of events and generations have already unfolded. Things like

Creation, Noah and the Flood, Abraham's covenant with God, and the Twelve Tribes of Israel through Jacob, Rachel, and Leah.

When we arrive in Exodus, we are in Egypt and there is a pharaoh (king) in charge who feels threatened by a group of people called the Israelites. Pharaoh was threatened by them because they worshiped Jehovah, the one true living God, the God you and I worship today. Pharaoh did not.

The Israelites began to multiply, and Pharaoh didn't like it. His solution? To oppress them by enslaving them to work for him and to command the midwives to kill any Israelite baby that was a boy (Exodus 1:8–17).

This didn't work because the midwives outsmarted Pharaoh, and so there was a new command from Pharaoh: any new baby boy was to be cast into the Nile River (Exodus 1:22).

Enter baby Moses.

His parents were smart. They hid him for three months, and then they did technically cast him into the Nile, as the command from Pharaoh was to be fiercely followed. However, Moses's mother carefully placed him in a waterproofed basket before putting him in the water.

Moses had a destiny on his life that nothing would stop, not even a Nile River filled with the most dangerous crocodiles, hippopotamuses, and venomous snakes. I am confident his momma's prayers kept him safe while he floated in the reeds of the river, where he would not only be rescued but would be restored to a life no one could have ever dreamed for him. From abandoned to adopted by royalty.

But this was only the beginning for Moses. He would later become the man God would choose to lead the Israelites out of Egypt. He would struggle with his own version of impostor syndrome, he would have excuses, and he would disobey, but God would use him from season to season in ways Moses could never imagine.

Transitions filled his life. Some he handled well. Some he did not. But every season was significant in his process with God. His process taught him lessons, gave him wisdom, and helped build strength to keep going. And the same will be true about your process with God.

> Through our process with God, we see problems, find promises, and in weakness find wisdom and strength through surrender.

Putting the Puzzle Together

For a few months before I began to write this book, I did something incredibly important to me as a communicator.

I spent some time just listening to the people in my life. I asked them intense questions about what transition looked like for them today. I collected all their responses, and a friend of mine organized them in a fancy spreadsheet.

Now, listen, normally spreadsheets make me want to break out in hives. But this one? It was like putting pieces of a puzzle together.

After I read the responses, I realized there were four transition categories most of us fell into despite our different circumstances. The emotions and questions the college graduate was facing were almost identical to the woman who went from being a stay-at-home mom to a working-outside-the-home mom. The responses of a woman trying to find her next job closely related to the woman who had just experienced a divorce. And the mom sending her first kid to kindergarten had responses almost identical to the woman who was about to get married. In the survey, circumstances varied but the individual underlying struggles of transition didn't.

The connections I found were through their process of transition, not the type of transition. So, I took those responses, emotions, struggles, and categories and grouped them into what I could identify as four seasons of transition: development, separation, cultivation, and finished.

Seasons are significant for so many reasons. Obviously, many places on earth go through four seasons: spring, summer, fall, and winter. You may see the correlation between the transition seasons and weather-type seasons throughout the book.

But how often do we think about our lives and the personal seasons we are in currently? Probably not until things are messy—we start to feel lost, confused, or shaken and begin to see the signs that a season has changed.

If we made a habit of taking the time to acknowledge where we are every day, it would help us learn to transition well.

Daily acknowledgment of where we are
would help us stop holding on to the past or
fearing the future and learn to embrace our now.

But just because we acknowledge something in our life is changing doesn't mean God won't allow life to toss unexpected things our way. And when we can see a potential transition coming, knowing how to prepare for it is one of the wisest things we can learn to do.

We are always in one of these four transition seasons, and getting ready for the next one. And the truth is, we may be in more than one transition season at the same time. Either way, it's important to know where you are currently.

We'll spend some time figuring out the days gone and the days to come, but for now, let's continue to settle into this season of your life, today. This is your new now.

Someone once said:
You didn't come this far to only come this far.

Your lifetime process with God has more to teach you.

On the next few pages, you'll find a detailed description of each of the four seasons of transition we'll use throughout this book. Keep this section dog-eared, or place a bookmark here so you can easily flip back to reread the descriptions if you need to throughout the book.

As you read through this next section, put a checkmark next to the season (or seasons) that best fits where you are today. But commit to studying each of the transition seasons and the life of Moses, because it will either help you see something you needed to gain from a previous season or help prepare you for what's coming during your next season of transition.

The Four Seasons of Transition

Transition Season One: Development

development—"the act or process of developing; growth; progress"[1]

Our farm, affectionately called the *Fixer Upper Farm*, is about twenty miles outside the center of Charlotte, North Carolina. Charlotte has been a booming city for decades now, but development has started creeping out to us.

Generational farms are being sold for a pretty penny, and new neighborhoods are being built everywhere we turn.

Developments always start with some type of clearing. Even if the trees are already knocked down on the land, there's still dirt and debris to clear before the land can be developed. And this happens so fast, right? Like one day we pass the field and it's got trees, fences, and barns on it. The next? Totally cleared.

Like a lot of seasons of transition, we may feel initially like we've been cleared out of something quickly. But once we accept we are in this season of transition, then we can begin the attempts to build or grow.

Multiple times we will see Moses in his own season of development and how this prepared him for what would ultimately come. But for this book, we'll focus mostly on his development through his birth and childhood.

Some ways to know if you are in this transition season:

- Most likely whatever transition you are experiencing came where someone else pointed out an area in you that needed development. For example, you didn't get the promotion/job because there is a skill or mindset that needs growth.
- Someone you care about pointed out something in your character that caused conflict in your relationship.
- People-pleasing has been a struggle for you, and you've made decisions based on the approval of others, which hasn't allowed you to become the truest version of yourself.

Transition Season Two: Separation

separation—"an act or instance of separating or the state of being separated"[2]

This is a hard transition season for most people. It's the space in time where we become separated from something or someone. Sometimes it's because of cruel circumstances, but other times it's a part of the process of our lives. This is the season where I learned that two common emotions of fear or anger can come out the strongest. But fear and anger don't have to transform us.

This can be one of the greatest seasons of refocusing on who we are and what really matters, if we will allow this separation place to teach us the lessons we need to learn.

To be clear, this transition isn't about separation from God, but it can feel as though He has exited our story for a time.

In the second section of this book, we will study how Moses went through a very clear season of separation from being a prince in the palace to a shepherd watching over sheep in a field. He also decided to separate himself as an Egyptian.

I don't think this was easy for him either, but it was necessary.

Some ways for you to identify if you are in this season of transition:

- You've moved to a new city. You had to leave friends and family behind, and there's an ache for people who are familiar. This ache doesn't seem to be fixed by anything.
- Someone you love dies, or a relationship that meant a lot to you ends. You find yourself looking back and longing for what was, but you know it can't be that way again.
- Something in your life, whether it's a sickness, pregnancy/birth, job change, or even a change of roles in your life, has caused you to pull away from things that once were your life.

Transition Season Three: Cultivation

cultivate—"to prepare and work on (land) in order to raise crops; till"[3]

For some people, this can be the most exciting season of transition.

If you can embrace this season of learning to cultivate things, it will make going from here to there much more thrilling. When we work through this season of transition in your life, I'll show you some daily habits we see in the Bible that are incredibly helpful to strengthen your faith, mind, and body.

We will see Moses go through a big season of cultivation midway through his life. You'll see how he pushed through and allowed this season to become one of his greatest teachers.

All of the seasons of transition are about change, but this is one where you can clearly see a change in your routine, habits, or calendar.

Some ways for you to identify if you are in this season:

- You get a new job or volunteer role that on paper you were qualified for (degree, certification, etc.), but you have to learn a whole new set of skills to actually do the position.
- God leads you into something new, but you don't have the funding, the experience, or the skills to do it.
- You desire something different in your life and know that it's going to take work to get there. This could be anything, like finishing a college degree, losing weight, or starting a ministry or business.

Transition Season Four: Finished

finished—"ended or completed"[4]

This will be the final transition season we will study in this book. We will learn the difference between quitting and finishing something well. Often a transition season of "finished" is hard to accept.

It doesn't mean something bad happened, you are not valuable anymore, or God is mad at you. It just means you have completed that place in your life and it's finished.

Moses had a messy finish to his assignment of leading the Israelites into the Promised Land. In fact, you'll see he didn't even get to go in. It's one of the saddest parts of this story, but Moses didn't quit. He finished well.

Some ways for you to know if you are in this transition season:

- What used to make you feel free now makes you feel frustrated.
- What worked well in one season of life no longer works well.
- God may be placing a new desire, dream, or even a burden to carry in your heart.
- You are out of ideas and options to keep things moving forward and just know you are done with this place in your life.

Still not sure what transition season you are in? Head to nickikoziarz.com/yournewnow to take the free assessment to help guide you through this.

2

Change for You

By faith Moses, when he was born, was hidden for three months by his parents, because they saw that the child was beautiful, and they were not afraid of the king's edict.

Hebrews 11:23

I've never met a first-time parent who didn't think their newborn baby was the most beautiful thing to ever grace planet earth. Me included. So imagine the shock I felt when someone came over for the first time to meet my newborn daughter and they said she looked like an alien.

And I wondered, *Where are my boxing gloves?*

Now, to be fair. I was a young *nineteen-year-old*. And so was this acquaintance. And neither of us had been around very many newborns. More than twenty years later, I can look back and kinda laugh at that comment.

Because honestly, some newborns, especially those with a rough birth process, do look a little like what Hollywood has told us aliens would look like.

So, as I'm reading Hebrews 11:23, I'm wondering... *Was Moses really that beautiful as a baby?* Or were his parents just over-the-moon in love with him and saw him as every parent should see their baby? Absolutely perfect.

David Guzik in his commentary about Exodus says, "Fanciful Jewish legends say that Moses' birth was painless to his mother, that at his birth his face was so beautiful that the room was filled with light equal to the sun and moon combined, that he walked and spoke when he was a day old, and that he refused to nurse, eating solid food from birth."[1]

I don't think all of this is true based on some things we'll see here in a minute. But still. Even baby Moses was a legend.

Hebrews 11:23 records, "By faith Moses, when he was born, was hidden for three months by his parents, because they saw that the child was beautiful, *and they were not afraid of the king's edict*" (emphasis mine).

I want us to focus on the part of this verse that says, "and they were not afraid of the king's edict."

Moses's parents didn't ask for this season of transition in their lives. They had intended to have a baby and raise him the way they did their other children. And through those nine words, we see how much had been developed in them already through this season of transition.

But imagine the fear, shock, and disbelief they held the day this announcement from Pharaoh hit their ears. Their "new now" began the day they heard this verdict. And I bet they felt a little like we do when we've been in a car accident, whiplashed and worn out.

In this chapter and the next, we're going to study the transition season of development. This is where we focus on learning the things we need to develop within us so that we can step into our next season confidently.

A Healthy Fear of God

Most transition seasons of development have some type of "fear of man" attached to them. This makes a development season hard to understand and overcome, because often God will use people to reveal what needs development within us.

Sometimes it comes in a really harsh form, like getting fired from a job or a Pharaoh making such a cruel law. Other times it comes a little more gently, such as a friend pointing out something unhealthy in our lives because they love us and want us to be better.

But at some point in each of our new nows, we have to stop fearing man, and fear God instead.

> The fear of man is crippling, but the fear of God is freeing—freeing us to develop.

Fearing God more than we fear man means at the end of the day, we're more concerned with how our Heavenly Father sees us than any earthly reflection can offer us.

Developing with God means we are committed to our growth process with Him. Even when it feels senseless, harsh, mean, or unfair (emphasis on *feels*). This space in our lives is crucial for our faith.

Moses's parents teach us that by having the fear of God deeply developed in us, we can be faithful, obedient, and inspiring despite anything that comes at us. They didn't just arrive at Pharaoh's verdict and then decide they were going to fear God more than man. This had been something building and developing in them through a lifetime of following God.

And whether your life of following after God has been short or long, it doesn't matter. If we aren't transitioning well from season to season and we feel stuck, lost, or skeptical about what God is doing, there's still something God needs to teach us.

A season of development can feel like a punishment. But it's not.

Development is a place of
divine preparation for what is coming next.

If you are not willing to develop, you won't develop. But if you are willing to develop, you will become wiser, stronger, and able to go from here to there with confidence.

The day Moses's parents placed him in the Nile was the moment the transition would have been complete. But during those three months they hid Moses, they were developing their souls for this risky act. Three months in the space between here and there, they were praying and preparing for what was coming.

Their preparation in the midst of this trying season would be the beginning of the miracle God was going to do through their son.

I don't know if the place you are in today will last three days, three months, or three years. No matter how hard the circumstances surrounding the transition you are going through, you can learn how to gracefully move from here to there.

You Are Not Here Because You Are Lost

Before we begin this next section, I need you to hear these words:

You are not lost.

Transition seasons often begin with a conversation in our heads trying to convince us we somehow missed a turn. And we're looking for the right direction, but we can't seem to see it.

I will not invalidate your feelings of being disoriented and off-course in your current season, but you are not lost.

As I've been sorting through all these changes happening in my life, I went to my husband in tears and said words I'm sure you've said too: *"I just feel so lost right now."*

Something has been so unsettled in me and I just couldn't seem to figure out what it was exactly.

> Feeling lost isn't a location where we
> wait to be found; it's a destination
> we need to be rescued from.

But as I would turn here or there, nothing seemed to come together or work out. I have even felt lost while writing these words in this book.

And I don't think I'm alone in this, because one of my really good friends just said to me the other day, *"Nicki, when I try to look into the future for me, I see nothing."*

She went on to say she sees a future for her husband and her kids, but she doesn't see anything for herself. I think that's what is so hard about this struggle. It can feel like everyone around you is getting married, graduating from college, sending their kids off to kindergarten or college, or moving up in their careers. And they are doing it so well.

The direction of their lives seems perfectly clear; they seem to know exactly where they are and where they are going.

As I'm writing this book, I am forty-one years old. I've been married for twenty-one years, and our girls are ages twenty-one, nineteen, and sixteen. The boys we are adopting are ages nine (twins) and six. My husband, Kris, and I bought a small, foreclosed farm just outside of Charlotte, North Carolina, nine years ago, and we've been restoring it year after year.

I've reached the point in my career as an author and speaker where I've started to wonder if this is what I will actually do for the rest of my life or if there's something different ahead. And honestly, this book and process I'm teaching you here on these pages might reveal that to me.

Those are scary, honest words to write.

This adoption has taken years, and I truly hope by the time these words make it into your hands, these boys are home with us. But it's hard to know for sure due to so much uncertainty surrounding this adoption. The process has been hard and painful at times. And so we're waiting in this in-between season, where I have felt lost.

I also lost half of my immediate family to tragic circumstances before the age of forty, and my dad moved to another state. I still haven't found a good rhythm for life during the holidays and other important dates. I feel lost without the family I've known my entire life. Those times of the year when we would normally be with family have also made me unsure I transitioned from that season well, because I often find myself during a holiday gathering slipping into the bathroom to wipe away tears of grief. I still wake up on my birthday wondering if my mom was the first to text me to wish me a happy birthday.

And just the other day, my dad was going through a little health scare and for some reason my initial reaction was to pull out my phone to text my brother to fill him in on what I thought I should do.

Just like you, I also lived through a worldwide pandemic from which we haven't fully recovered. Life felt like it was canceled for a significant amount of time, and it's been hard to find our places again in the community, at gatherings, and even church.

If you feel lost in life right now, I can relate, more than I would like to admit.

I understand what it feels like to wake up day after day and feel as though you are in some time warp, much like the movie *Groundhog Day.* You want to move ahead and get out of this season because it doesn't feel good, it's obnoxious at times, and it feels as though so many days are being wasted. Maybe you keep waking up and it's the same thing again and again.

But the Lord taught me some hard lessons about this place of transition, and one of them is to stop saying, "I feel lost." Because every time I say those words, I give myself permission to stay stuck and not get what I need out of this season.

Acknowledge that this is a weird place of life, yes. But decide that you are going to grow, gain wisdom, and find the truth of what God needs you to see in this place.

Say this with me:

I'm not lost, I'm learning the way.

But how do we learn what we need to learn?

This feels like a really good time for us to start digging a little deeper into this first transition season of *development*.

When Someone Tells You to Develop

One of the most interesting jobs I've ever had was being a unit secretary at a hospital in the cardiac unit. A few weeks after I began my job, the hospital rolled out a new leadership initiative program and required us to fill out these annoying weekly forms and meet with the head nurse of the unit on a consistent basis so they could evaluate our performance. No one enjoyed this, and I wasn't seeing many positive things come through the process. Everyone was complaining and rolling their eyes about this new initiative.

One night, I came in for my shift and had a short conversation with the day-shift secretary to get the unit report for the day. After her report was done, she looked at me with tears in her eyes and said, *"Well, they're putting me into a season of development."*

I knew exactly what she meant. And it was something we all feared.

This new system was catching our administrative errors, and we were being held accountable for mistakes. They were right to do so, but the entire process felt very harsh.

If you were put into a season of development, it meant more meetings with the head nurse that everyone knew about, more personal evaluations, more looking over your shoulder, and more boring training videos to watch.

Basically, it was a *three-more-strikes-and-you're-out* situation.

Unfortunately, she didn't stop striking out, and very soon there was a job posting for a day-shift unit secretary up on the hospital website. As my fellow unit secretary transitioned out of this position, which she had held for so many years, there was a lot of frustration.

In fact, as my job continued, I saw a pattern. Most of the people who were put into this development process didn't make it out.

Here's the truth.

Sometimes people don't want to get better.

And when they feel as though they don't measure up in someone's eyes, they can spiral to a place of self-defeat. There's surely some fancy psychological term for this, but I'm sure you can think of someone in your life who has experienced this too. Maybe a few of us would even be willing to raise our hands and say, "Yes, I've spiraled into self-defeat too."

Because of that negative experience with being developed professionally, when I hear people say things like, "You are in a season of development," anxious thoughts can enter in.

It makes me feel like I may lose something I really love. Or worse, I might lose something I need, like a job.

I bet if you and I were sitting face-to-face right now, you could share with me a time someone showed you an area in your life, whether personally or professionally, that needed to be developed. I would guess you would tell me that at first it felt stressful, confusing, or maybe you even got a little angry.

And I'd be curious to know how that place in your life actually turned out. Did it make you better or did it make you bitter?

When You Are the Boss

Today, I don't have a boss asking for weekly meetings or for me to fill out a check-in form. I start and stop my days when I want to. And to a certain extent, it is great. I love the flexibility of what I do.

But as a full-time, self-employed woman, no one actually cares how I spend my time. And no one cares if I improve my skills. No one is going to put me into a season of development.

Maybe you are also your own boss or there's no one in front of you asking for a weekly meeting, forcing you to watch a training video, read a leadership book, or do something to improve yourself. And from the stay-at-home mom to the entrepreneur, or to the person who sits behind a desk for a company that cares more about results than development, we can easily get ourselves into a bad place mentally.

Because it can feel as though no one cares if you win or fail.

So, how do you step confidently into the next season of life with your head held high if you don't even know what's keeping your head down?

Here's the good news.

Whether you punch a time clock or if no one knows your daily schedule . . . you have a CEO of your life: God. And He cares incredibly much about your process with Him.

One day we will all be held accountable to Him for what we do in this lifetime. As 2 Corinthians 5:10 says, "For we must all appear before the judgment seat of Christ, so that each one may receive what is due for what he has done in the body, whether good or evil."

I didn't want to put that verse above on these pages so early into this process for you, because it can feel harsh just pulled from Scripture without any loving context. That phrase "judgment seat" doesn't really make anyone feel good, nor does it sound like something to look forward to.

And since there's a possibility your life feels a little unkind to you today, the thought of one day being "judged" for all this crud in your life today could feel a little nauseating.

But what I need us to agree on is that this is a temporary place we are in. These struggles we have here as humans will one day end and we will stand before God.

> Transition is temporary,
> but a life of following Jesus is eternal.

There are two things we are guaranteed to have as humans: a birth date and a death date. And whether thinking about this makes us feel good or second-guess our life decisions, it's the reality of life.

What we do with our lives today matters. So, if we are not moving from season to season well in our lives, we could be wasting time, energy, emotions, and opportunity.

This is why it's good to recognize when we're in a transition season of development and do what we need to do today. Then, we can get to tomorrow and know we have done our part to develop ourselves for whatever God has for us.

Signs of a Transition Season of Development

I shared in the previous chapter that there are external signs of a new season all around me. In each of these transition seasons we are discussing, the internal signs of change are there too.

In a transition season of development, most likely we have been cleared or are being cleared from something. Perhaps the clearing started slowly, maybe it was even unrecognizable, but then it was superfast. Remember the example I gave in the previous chapter about how neighborhood developments begin? One day you're driving past a farm field; there are behind-the-scenes plans to develop the land that we know nothing about. And then one day we drive past again, and every tree, barn, and fence has been knocked down.

Seasons of development can feel so similar to us. We can find ourselves asking things like, "How did this happen?" "How did I get here?" or "What did I miss?"

And what you will see later on is that this transition season is unique because there is a place inside us that feels like suffering. Think again of Moses's parents not knowing the outcome of their choice. Placing that baby in the Nile River must have literally taken their breath away in grief, because they had no idea how it would turn out. It was their own *new now*.

We could easily mistake this season as a place of failure, but it's not. The positive side of a transition season of development is that it holds the opportunity for growth, progress, and positive change in our lives.

Development can actually be a place we learn to enjoy. But first, let's talk about how we got here.

Examples of ways we can enter into a transition season of development:

- We experience conflict (Ex: not working on our communication or conflict management, and relationships start to end).

- We don't have clear boundaries (Ex: unfair expectations others have put on us or saying too many yeses and not being able to keep up).
- We stop learning or keeping up with the changes in our world (Ex: most jobs and life skills require training to keep up with technology or social media trends).
- We don't fully understand who we are, and so we're constantly trying to please others (Ex: the volunteer who held on to a position for years just to make the leader happy and never worked on their other skills).
- We waste time (Ex: if we're given a task and we chase shiny things all day and don't complete the task).
- We don't recognize our own places of weakness (Ex: entering into a place of sin in our lives).
- We fear the future, so never take steps to prepare for it (Ex: a college student graduating with a degree without much thought about employment—and now they are afraid they don't even want to use that degree).

When we are in a space between here and there in our life and the above list is ringing a little too true, most likely we are in a transition season of development. Recognizing this season is one thing; coming through it better than you were before is another.

Just like the unit secretary at the hospital who wasn't willing to do what she needed to do to keep her job, this is where we have to get humble and seek the truth of what's happening.

Have you ever heard a court news reporter say something like, *"I'm here today with some developing news around the case of Sally Sue"*? In this transition season of development, we need to do some investigating of our own.

In the next chapter, we will consider your childhood to see if we can see any clues as to where you are today. Maybe we'll discover some clues that will help you understand why you feel the way you do about this transition in your life.

But as we close this chapter, I have some tasks and questions for you. Whether or not you feel as though you are currently in a transition season of development, this activity will help you gain wisdom for the seasons past and the seasons to come.

1. Write a prayer to God. Get honest with Him about this season you are in. Ask Him to reveal what you need to see, change, and shift in your life.

2. Make a list of at least three things you can look back on over your life that you've already developed. Think back to your childhood, previous jobs, or roles in life you've seen growth in. (The purpose of this is to remind your soul that you *can* develop. And it's good for you.)

3. Make a list of at least three areas you see need to be developed within you.

4. Ask someone you trust and who knows you very well to look over that list with you. Give them permission to be honest and authentic about things you sense need developing. Listen to their feedback, and make any needed changes to your list.

5. Create a plan of action of what you need to do to experience growth in those places.

6. Do those things on your action list. Repeat as many times as necessary until you feel released spiritually from this place.

7. Keep a record of anything you see as evidence of progress.

PS: If you are a person who loves to have some type of worksheet to do this, head to nickikoziarz.com/freebies and download your own season of development worksheet.

3

Delayed Developments

> When the child grew older, she brought him to Pharaoh's
> daughter, and he became her son. She named him Moses,
> "Because," she said, "I drew him out of the water."
>
> Exodus 2:10

After Moses's parents obeyed Pharaoh's command to place the baby boy in the Nile River, we see something miraculous happen. What unfolds is the result of a posture of fearing God, in a good way.

Moses is floating, floating, and floating in the Nile River among the reeds in a papyrus basket. There is a connection between the Hebrew word used here in the Scriptures for *basket* to Noah and the Ark. In both of these biblical accounts we see that the fear of God brings the safety of God.

Pharaoh's daughter sees the papyrus basket in the reeds, she hears the cries of this baby, and immediately God does something in her heart. Once she opens the basket, she realizes this baby is a Hebrew. This could have been because he was circumcised or because her father had commanded that the Hebrew baby boys be placed in the river. Because she had been trained her whole life to despise the Hebrew people, we see a beautiful example of God doing something undeniable.

> God can use even the most unlikely people
> to help bring us from here to there.

This woman doesn't worship the same God the family of Moses does. And yet God chose her.

This story teaches us that when we are in a place of transition requiring us to develop, we can overlook the very people God wants to use in our lives. We can easily discount people because they don't look like us, talk like us, or even believe the way we do.

I almost missed what God was doing through someone who crossed my path in my own transition season of development.

When to Engage and When to Exit

Each Thursday night for almost an entire year, about twenty-five young adults would arrive at my house at 7:00 p.m. We would gather each week to study something interesting about the Bible as it related to the world we were living in. The group was so fun, and I always looked forward to our intense but healthy discussions.

One night, a new guy entered the living room, and immediately he started having some weird reactions toward our group. He seemed very skeptical and uneasy about being in a group setting. But we all did our best to make him feel welcome.

I'm not sure where the breakdown in communication happened, but for some reason he thought our church practiced something called Omnism. Meaning, the belief in all religions and gods.

That night, he questioned me about the Bible, very intensely and argumentatively in front of the entire group. I listened and tried my best to answer his questions, but honestly, I just wanted him out of my house because he just seemed argumentative.

That night became one of the greatest places of development for me. Only it would be years later, a delay of sorts, until I would understand what had been developed in me.

The season of this group meeting at my home was getting ready to end. I knew a transition for the group and myself was coming. And wow, was this situation making that decision to end the group easier.

We ended the night, and I walked this young man out, barely saying goodbye. I could tell he felt bad for the way he drilled me, and I'll be truthful, my first reaction was one of offense.

> When our reaction to others is one of
> offense, we can either learn from it or
> let it go, not for them, but for us.

Later that night as I lay in bed tossing and turning over his questions, I realized if I was ever going to move to a place in ministry where I was able to reach people in my living room and beyond, I would have to learn to embrace these types of conversations.

The next day, I sent him an email.

I thanked him for his bravery in coming to the group and explained that the group was actually coming to an end soon. But I told him I welcomed his questions and would be more than willing to discuss things further with him and a pastor if he wanted to.

He declined and said ours was the wrong church for him. But he did thank me for being willing to talk to him.

All these years later, the development God did in me is still there. Because whenever I teach or write something publicly, I think of him.

As I grow in ministry, it seems I encounter more people with beliefs like his. Sometimes the emails and comments that come in feel harsh. But instead of just seeing those conversations to the door, I have developed a process within me.

First, I listen. And then, I listen some more. And then I ask this question: "Tell me—what brought you to this place of asking this question?" Most of the time that helps me see their heart.

Are they just curious or seeking? Or have they been hurt in the past by someone in the Church? Normally the response to that question reveals something that helps me have a better reaction than just being offended by their words.

If I can answer it, I do. And if I can't, I don't try. I have learned over the years that sometimes people just want to argue. Being able to discern how to handle hard questions was developed in me years ago, but it's something I've recently recognized. This delayed development from that transition in my life has helped me know when to engage and when to exit.

Whether it's an unlikely woman like Pharaoh's daughter picking up a miracle baby in a river, or someone showing up in your own living room—

May we never discount the people God sends our way to help us develop in a season of transition.

While Pharaoh's daughter is stepping into her new season of adoptive mom, there's someone watching: Moses's sister, Miriam. The bravery of his sister at this moment isn't something to be overlooked. She knew when to engage and she knew when to exit. And when the time was just right, she popped up and asked Pharaoh's daughter a brilliant question:

Then his sister said to Pharaoh's daughter, "Shall I go and call you a nurse from the Hebrew women to nurse the child for you?" And Pharaoh's daughter said to her, "Go." So the girl went and called the child's mother.

Exodus 2:7–8

Not only did Moses's sister get a front-row seat to watch this process for Moses unfold, but she also became the key to one of the greatest blessings Moses's mother would experience.

What if Pharaoh's daughter had discounted Miriam as just a nosey child? Instead, she was able to report back to her mom that not only was Moses alive, he'd been rescued by a princess.

But it got even better. Moses's mother was about to get paid to nurse her own baby.

And Pharaoh's daughter said to her, "Take this child away and nurse him for me, and I will give you your wages." So the woman took the child and nursed him.

Exodus 2:9

What a powerful story of what can happen when a woman decides she fears God more than she fears man.

> When God steps in and changes hearts, it is for our benefit.

Take a minute and think through the past few years of your life. Are there any people you discounted, but now you can see God was using them to help you develop? As you think back on that experience, what is something you learned from that unexpected source?

Part of the beauty of something being developed in our lives and not seeing or recognizing it until later on is that it unveils the glory of God's timeline, not ours. God can redeem today the lessons we missed in the past.

It may feel like a delayed development, but it is still valid.

Moses Grows Up

One day, when Moses had grown up, he went out to his people and looked on their burdens, and he saw an Egyptian beating a Hebrew, one of his people.

Exodus 2:11

One of the clearest seasons of development we can see in the life of Moses is his childhood. We may never fully understand some of the hard things about his life as he transitioned from papyrus-basket baby to prince of Egypt, because the Bible doesn't contain a lot of details about this season.

We know that Pharaoh's palace wasn't just a playground for a curious boy. It was a training ground for a boy to become a man. But we see something interesting in Exodus 2:11. It says that as Moses had grown up, he knew the Hebrew people were his people.

But, how? Perhaps one of the reasons Moses knew he was a Hebrew was because he was circumcised. Also, Moses was most likely with his mother nursing until age three. Did she use every moment of those formative years to tell him exactly who he was? Did he remember? Or was he treated differently by Pharaoh because of his daughter's mercy on him?

We won't ever know all the details, but Acts 7:22 tells us this: "And Moses was instructed in all the wisdom of the Egyptians, and he was mighty in his words and deeds."

This is comforting to me for several reasons.

One, as a mom and mentor to others, it reminds me that no matter what evil influence surrounds my family or the people I pour into, God's plan is bigger than the enemy's schemes.

> God can even use places of evil influence
> as a training ground for our future.

But second, it reveals that despite anything in my own childhood the enemy attempted to use for his purpose, God does not even shudder at his attempts.

> God can take a complicated past
> and use it simply for His glory.

I'm walking through this right now with one of my kids. The enemy has done a work, but I see past it. I see the future and hope mentioned in verses like Jeremiah 29:11 in this situation. And even today I am comforted by this place Moses experienced in his life. How he could be surrounded by false truth, lies, deception, and pure evil in Pharaoh's palace, and yet this was what God used to develop him.

Unfortunately for Moses, forty years of development in the palace wouldn't be enough. We'll see in the next section that Moses would stay in development—and also enter into a transition season of separation—for another forty years. (Remember I mentioned you can be in more than one of these seasons at the same time? You'll see that next.)

But maybe someone is reading this right now thinking, *I don't have that much time. I need to get this right, right now.* I'm glad you feel that urgency, and it gives me hope for our process together. But—

> In God's kindness, He will let us stay here
> until we develop what we need to develop.

So let's look back on some things we may have missed to help keep us moving forward.

Rethinking Your Childhood

My childhood taught me much about adaptability. My dad was a teacher for the government, so I spent a big portion of my growing-up years in two different countries: Germany and Japan.

Learning to navigate new cultures, and so many different people transitioning in and out of my life at a young age, taught me the need to be able to adapt to an environment and people. Because of this, I can walk into almost any environment and change who I tend to naturally be based on what I'm feeling in the room. It's a strength called adaptability.

This last week I caught myself using this strength.

I tend to be a bubbly person and unafraid to meet people for the first time. But last week, when I sat at a table with someone I'd never met in person before, I could see right away she wasn't a bubbly person at all. And, she looked a little terrified to meet me.

Instinctively I knew to act differently. And so, I brought my tone and body language down to hers. She immediately felt more at ease, and I could tell what the table conversation needed that day.

Other times I'll walk into the room with a very high-energy person, and I just know to bring my energy up to their level to make them feel at ease. Sometimes this feels exhausting, always trying to read the room and meet people where they are, but I also believe it's a gift my childhood gave me to be able to do this. This was something good that was developed in me without me having to take a class or read a book.

The little version of you has clues as to why you are the way you are today.

No matter if your childhood was really hard or really good, there are gifts God placed in you from your childhood to help you face your current battles.

We're going to see in the next chapter how the little version of Moses affected grown-up Moses, but for the rest of this chapter, let's spend some time thinking about you.

Remember, this first season we are studying is about development. And while life today offers you many development opportunities, your past has some clues as to why you may react to transition the way you do. If you liked the way you feel about the transitions happening in your life, I'm not sure you'd be reading this book.

Most likely you want to be better about this.

When we sense we need some development in our lives—or we could say, some *growing up* in an area of our lives—it would be very normal to go into a conversation with a therapist or pastor about these struggles.

I am neither of those, and I would encourage you to seek professional help if this book doesn't seem to help you. But I have done what I'm about to tell you with multiple counselors and pastors.

Typically, in a counseling session a therapist will begin to understand you by asking questions like I've included below. They do this to help understand where you came from and why you might react the way you do.

Since you and I are not face-to-face working through these questions, I would encourage you to pull out a journal and take a few of these questions and process them.

Or, write your answers here in this book. But for real, don't just skip over this. If we're going to get you to a healthy place in the midst of your transitions, we have to do the work.

- Who was your primary caregiver? And what was your relationship like with them?
- What were the things you were afraid of?
- What is your most vivid memory?

- What is a smell or sound that reminds you of your childhood?
- What were some of the things that made you happy?
- How were you disciplined?
- What were you taught about God?
- How did you express your emotions?
- What were some of the values you were raised to believe?
- What did you play as a child? Do you see any connection from your childhood play to who you are today? (Ex: If you played school, do you teach?)
- Do you remember any specific words (positive or negative) someone said to you?
- How were your friendships?

If you've answered these questions, you've started the process of acknowledging your past. But wait, there's more.

Now, after looking over those responses, what connections do you see with your life and your reactions today? Think about if you feel like you were fully developed in those places from your childhood. Or are you experiencing some reactions in the midst of this current transition that indicate you are experiencing a delayed development in an area?

Here's an example from my own life.

When I was working through those questions, one of the things that stuck out to me was the question about friendships. Because I moved so much as a child, sometimes it's been hard for me to stay connected with people long-term.

Especially when I'm in a transition.

When one season ends and I see a new one ahead, it's hard for me to believe the people in the prior season can go with me into the next. Before I had this realization, I cut off relationships left and right when the transition came.

But now that I see it, it hurts my soul to think about the people whose friendships I miss. As a child I never developed the process of being able to move into a new season of life and remain friends with someone. Understanding this about myself is the beginning of developing this ability in me. It's a delayed development, but it's still a development. What is something you can see as a potential delayed development in your life that could have stemmed from your childhood?

Let's go back and revisit the initial definition of *development* I gave you:

noun
   the act or process of developing; growth; progress

If you are sensing you haven't gone through the full process of growth and progress in a specific area, it's time to recognize it. Sometimes we can't figure out why we feel stuck or lost because we never dealt with the things that didn't finish developing in us.

For some of you, I know this is painful.

Nothing in you wants to look back on your childhood. And there are some parts of my life that I don't want to look back on either and will never make it into a book. I understand.

But for others, maybe this caused an ache because life was good for you as a child. Looking back makes you long for the way things were and those people you miss in your life again.

Often we tend to dwell in the memory of the past because it makes the reality of today disappear.

I'm a believer in counseling, reflection, and asking yourself the hard questions, but mostly I am a believer in prayer. And sometimes I think the best way we can transition well from one season to the next is by breaking off the things that weigh us down from the past.

**Prayer can change our wounds to scars
and allow the past to heal, not destroy.**

Below is a prayer I've prayed for breakthrough for those things in my life that still need to be developed from past seasons. I'm facing this struggle head-on, and I know that prayer is a weapon to fight for the wellness of our souls.

You don't need to walk an aisle in a church and have someone lay hands on you to experience breakthrough. Right now, you and God alone wherever you are, at the gym, in your car, on your sofa or in your bed, can experience this.

A Prayer for Breakthrough in a Season of Development

God, as I think of my past and the places You have faithfully brought me through, I am grateful. Thank You for Your kindness, mercy, and grace for my process with You. I see, Lord, there are still some areas in my life that need development.

And so right now, I bring my childhood wounds, my past doubts, the fear I've had of man more than You, and the places I've just been disobedient, into Your presence. Show me what I need to see.

Forgive me, Lord, for the places I have wronged You and haven't been obedient to this process.

Help me to receive Your forgiveness and stop replaying these places in my life that keep me stuck. Show me what I need to see, and then help me march ahead.

By the power of Jesus, I cancel out the enemy's plan to discourage and distract me from these places in my life. I call forward the authority given to me by the power of the cross and declare that today is a day I become aware of Your plans and purpose for me.

I am becoming wiser and stronger because of what You are teaching me today. Holy Spirit, lead me to the place of breakthrough through this transition season of development in my life. In the name of Jesus, Amen, let it be.

In-Between-Seasons Mini Bible Study

At the end of each section of this book, you have the opportunity to take your own study of Moses a little deeper. I highly recommend doing this portion so you can fully grasp the story of Moses. And if you're reading this book in a group setting, this is a great place to have some discussion each time you meet.

It's good for us to know where we are picking up in the Scriptures whenever we begin to study a story from the Bible. Below are some Bible timeline events that will be helpful for you to remember as we enter into Exodus.

Use the box below and fill in the timeline event based on the verse.

Genesis 1:1	Genesis 5:5–6	Genesis 37:28
Genesis 3:6–7	Genesis 11:3	Genesis 49:28

Tower of Babel	Sin enters humanity	The Flood
12 Tribes of Israel are blessed by Jacob (Israelites)	Joseph is sold by his brothers, goes to Egypt	Creation

The above timeline helps us understand how the Israelites ended up in Egypt.

Read Exodus 1–2

Who is the author of Exodus?

    a. Jacob

    b. David

    c. Moses

Read Genesis 15:12–16

This passage is where we see the prophetic promise from God to Abraham about the future of the Israelites. The land mentioned here is Egypt, and where God is telling Abraham they will return to is Canaan, otherwise referred to as the Promised Land.

All of Exodus is the process of God fulfilling this promise.

What were your thoughts about the midwives' actions mentioned in Exodus 1:17–21?

Were there any words you read in Exodus 1 and 2 that you need to define or pay attention to? If yes, use the space below to look the words up using a website like biblehub.com.

Ex: The word *Exodus* means *going out, departure*.

Study note: often you will see Moses's people referred to by two names:

1. The Hebrews
2. The Israelites

Do you know why? Yes or No

Here's some insight on this: *Israelite* is a designation of them as a nation descended from one man, Israel (Jacob). *Hebrew* is less clear and seems to refer to ethnicity. No one is quite sure of the origin of the term, but it was first used in the Bible in Genesis 14:13, where it was applied to Abraham. There are several possible derivations, such as someone descended from Eber (Genesis 11:14–17), or possibly someone who had crossed the river, meaning the Euphrates, which would describe him as an immigrant.

Most scholars are more inclined to believe the first one. But in any event, it came to describe the ethnicity of Abraham and all his descendants. But Abraham was not an Israelite, because it was his grandson Jacob (Israel) who was the origin of the nation of Israel. Then the term Israelite came to be used after the descendants of Jacob (Israel) were numerous enough and distinct enough from others that they were seen as belonging to the nation of Israel.

Write down your main takeaway from reading Exodus 1–2 and this section of the book:

_____

_____

_____

_____

_____

_____

_____

_____

_____

_____

SEPARATION

4

When It's Time to Separate

When we hear the word *separation*, a variety of emotions are evoked. One, it can feel negative. Such as, my friend is separating from her husband. Or two, it can feel a little juvenile, right? As in the teacher had to separate the students because they wouldn't stop arguing.

And maybe you are thinking, *I am in neither of those categories.* But let me ask you a few questions:

1. Have you ever felt (or do you currently feel) God is allowing you to be removed from someone or something?
2. Do you understand what it's like to have been close with someone (a child, coworker, friend, etc.) and they are suddenly not by your side anymore?
3. Have you been a part of something that suddenly changes direction, and you are no longer needed there or do not want to be there?

4. Has a season of sickness, pregnancy/birth, or an injury caused you to have to pull away from the things you normally do?
5. Did you experience some type of conflict or hurt in a relationship, and you are no longer part of that person's life?

If you answered *yes* to any of these questions, it is possible you have experienced what it's like to be in a transition season of separation. And many of us may currently be right here. This may just be our *new now*.

Whether or not you are currently experiencing separation or a past memory feels fresh in your mind, it's possible this season of life still needs to teach you something about where you have been or where you are going next.

In the previous section, we unpacked the transition season of development, and one of the core feelings about that type of season was feeling lost. And while there are a slew of emotions and feelings a transition season of separation can bring, one of the central emotions seems to be loneliness.

Deep loneliness has been a part of every transition season of separation I've walked through—from the time I graduated from high school and watched all my friends go off to a four-year college, while I stayed behind to attend a community college, to the day I had to leave my kids at childcare and go to an office job for the first time. Separation *never* makes me feel like I've got a bunch of cheerleaders by my side.

The crazy thing about feeling alone is that you can be surrounded by people all day long and still feel isolated. Because while we might have people by our side, they may not be the people we want ... or the people that *used* to be there.

If this is where you are today, I want to recognize that you may feel the most alone you've ever felt. There's an ache that no amount of social media scrolling, conversations filled with fluff, or activities can fill.

You feel alone, and I agree with what you're feeling; it's real. But this isn't where we are staying. We're not going to let this sense of isolation keep us stuck much longer. There are a few lessons we need to learn, and then, we will move along. This isn't permanent, but this is our process.

Why God Lets Us Experience This

As his heart monitor flat-lined, it was the most alone I've ever felt.

Standing in an ICU room overlooking the city of Seattle, Washington, I watched my brother, my only brother, die from the destructive choices he made. His life transitioned from here to eternity, and the cruel irony of this moment was that I had dropped everything to fly as quickly as possible from Charlotte to Seattle, just so he wouldn't have to die alone. And yet now that he was gone, I was the most alone I'd ever felt.

I looked at his arm, which had a tattoo of a lion that appeared swollen from the IV in his arm. His roaring battle was truly done. And I was left in the aftermath of sorting through his sudden death.

My tear-filled eyes and angry soul were drawn to the window. The rare appearance of the fall sun was setting across the city. Shadows from the buildings, with beams from the sun's streams of light poured through. And there were two white birds circling in front of the window. Again and again.

Too obvious to not believe God was trying to get my attention, this verse came to mind: *When you pass through the waters, I will be with you* (Isaiah 43:2).

For a moment, I didn't feel so alone.

There was a presence in that room with me, and in the hard days to come, that was undeniably God. And although God went with me, it didn't stop what was to come. A hard season of separation had begun for me, and grief is one of the unkindest experiences that can lead us into this season.

And while I craved the arms of my husband or the presence of my daughters at that moment, I had what I needed. Not what I wanted, the tangible presence of my family, but what I needed most: God's presence.

In transition seasons of separation, it can appear that God is being unkind to us. We will see in the next few pages what can lead us into this season and how Moses got there too.

There are some hard truths we need to learn, and I want to warn you that your soul may resist this. We often work hard to not feel the things we need to feel. I know, I'm the queen of wanting to escape the reality of hard situations.

God has a purpose in all our seasons of life, but this season's lessons are among the most important:

God may not be all we want, but He is all we need.

This is a temporary place, but it is filled with temptations that can lead to permanent problems if we don't seek this wisdom-filled lesson in this season. Here are a few questions for you to answer as we continue to identify this place in your life:

1. What is the most alone you've ever felt?

2. Do you see a transition attached to those feelings? If so, what is or was the transition?

3. Who were the people you wanted to be there with you during that time of your life?

4. How did you view God during that time? Be as honest as possible.

Defining a Transition Season of Separation

The transition season of separation can catch us off guard. Maybe we thought we would never be here, trying to figure this all out and feeling alone. Maybe we thought the mentor, spouse, friend, coworker, or whoever or whatever it is, would always be there.

When God allows us to enter the transition place of separation, it's not because He's punishing us. Instead, He's proving to us that He is what we need. Everything and everyone else will fail us at some point. He won't.

Let's process a few more transition seasons of separation scenarios before we move on to our study of Moses.

Here are some more possibilities that can bring us to this season of transition:

- Friendships, for whatever reason, end.
- Someone close to you dies; this grief is one of the hardest separations.
- You worked in an office surrounded by coworkers, and now you work at home, alone.
- The dating relationship didn't turn into marriage, and your Facebook status is once again "single."
- You may temporarily separate from a spouse or go through a permanent one, divorce.
- Kids go to preschool, kindergarten, middle/high school, and then college or start a career.
- You get promoted or demoted, and no longer have the same coworkers.
- You go from stay-at-home mom to working mom or vice versa.
- You move to a new city, state, or country.

> A transition season of separation
> isn't always a negative thing, but when it happens,
> it's always a necessary thing.

And listen, some people thrive through transition and there are no struggles. But I suspect they aren't the ones picking up this book. And the feeling of isolation isn't the only thing that can taunt us in a season like this. There's something else there too—*sin.*

One of Moses's Biggest Mistakes

When we left off with our study of Moses in the last section of the book, he was transitioning from a child into a man. He was also beginning to embrace who he was as a Hebrew.

I would tend to believe he spent a good bit of these transition years asking this question: *Who am I?*

Sometimes when that question cannot be answered authentically because everything we've known is no more, it can cause us to make decisions that shock even us. Which is about to happen with Moses.

Acts 7:23 tells us that the next scene of Moses's life unfolds at the age of forty.

Moses looked out at this Hebrew hate culture his grandfather, Pharaoh, had created and was deeply grieved by it. And so, at some point in Moses's growing-up process, he had made a decision to no longer identify as one of the Egyptians. Read this with me:

> By faith Moses, when he was grown up, refused to be called the son of Pharaoh's daughter, choosing rather to be mistreated with the people of God than to enjoy the fleeting pleasures of sin. He considered the reproach of Christ greater wealth than the treasures of Egypt, for he was looking to the reward.
>
> Hebrews 11:24–26

In a way, Moses put himself into his own transition season of separation. He made the decision that he no longer wanted to be under Pharaoh's rule.

And isn't that a powerful message for you and me?

As you reflected on your childhood in the last section of the book, I'm sure you identified some things you wished weren't part of your process or identity. But just because you grew up with beliefs you would identify as "wrong" or "unjust" doesn't mean you have to keep them.

> We can either dwell in roots of destruction
> or choose to separate so that we grow
> into who God wants us to be.

I wish we could study more of Moses's process from a child to a man. But the Scriptures don't tell us anything else than what I've shared. Next in Moses's story, we see a wave of anger stirring in him that obviously stems from this transition season of separation he is in.

> One day, when Moses had grown up, he went out to his people and looked on their burdens, and he saw an Egyptian beating a Hebrew, one of his people. He looked this way and that, and seeing no one, he struck down the Egyptian and hid him in the sand.
>
> Exodus 2:11-12

And just like that, Moses enters into a place of sin. One of his greatest mistakes (unfortunately there are more coming) happens in this moment, and boom . . . this becomes the defining moment of him entering into a transition season of separation.

We aren't so different from Moses. When we watch years of injustice unfold around us and we have finally had enough, it can cause all kinds of reactions within us. Some bad, some good.

We don't know if when Moses saw his fellow Hebrew being beaten, he just couldn't take it anymore, or if he just fell into a very human reaction of *eye for an eye.*

Moses knew killing the Egyptian was wrong, because the text says that he was literally looking to his left and his right to make sure no one saw what he was doing (Exodus 2:12). His need to fight for justice isn't what was wrong, it was his impulsive decision and the hiding.

This is one of those moments in time when Moses thought he was alone. He thought he could get away with his actions. And sometimes who we are when we think no one is looking becomes the place where we make those shocking decisions.

How Do You React When No One Sees?

Most of my brother's destructive decisions came from a season when he was separated from his wife, kids, and our family. He admitted this place of separation made him feel more alone and isolated. So, when no one was looking, the drugs and alcohol became his escape.

Sometimes a season of separation can make us feel like we need to escape reality, somehow, someway. So, for me, it's easy to turn to TV or social media and allow myself to completely escape the reality of the hard, lonely places. I just want to turn my brain off and not deal with the way I feel. This causes me to be unintentional with my time, and before I know it, hours of my life are often wasted.

But hiding and escaping from life and God doesn't work.

Whether God feels near or far, He is still seeking us out, calling us higher, and waiting for us to see Him as the answer to our sin struggles.

None of us are exempt from the temptation to do things we wouldn't normally do when we think no one is looking. It's why Eve ate the fruit, David looked at Bathsheba, Judas betrayed Jesus, and the list goes on and on.

What brings us ultimately to a place of separation from God is our sin. And I hate to write things like this, because normally I'm your cheerleader author friend shouting things like YOU CAN DO HARD THINGS!

But man, maybe it's just this season I'm in, or the emotional garbage I see all around me today, but sin always leads to some type of separation.

First, it separates us from God, then it separates us from others, and then if it's not dealt with, it can separate us from the truest version of who God created us to be.

And before we know it, our identity can become shaped by sin.

The hardest thing about sin is it's so sneaky. Slipping in when we least expect it, catching us off guard. It can also be something that becomes part of our routine.

I think about Moses and how many times he probably tried to do the right thing.

The conversations he must have had to fight for justice for the Hebrew people. The prayers he possibly prayed for God to do something. The snappy comments he might have thought about saying to Pharaoh.

But then I am sure there were those times when his anger rose up in such a way that perhaps he entertained the thought of hurting an Egyptian for what they were doing to his people.

Ultimately, Moses would make a decision that would become the leading scene for his transition season of separation.

These struggles aren't just about a space in time in our lives. Whether you are in a transition season of separation or not, there's something tempting your faithfulness to God. I encourage you to call out that place in your life. Don't let it stay hidden.

Call sin what it is: sin. But then call on the name of Jesus, because His name holds the power and authority to break every sin off our lives.

> **We do not have to allow one destructive thought to turn into a life-changing destructive decision.**

But can I be honest?

I think this is something the Christian community and the Church doesn't like to talk about. Myself included. But it's so necessary.

Just like almost every day there's something in my house that needs to be cleaned up, there's also something in my soul that needs a daily process of cleaning up. And it doesn't have to be this long, drawn-out, or overwhelming thing.

After reflecting on our day, it can simply be praying something like this:

God, help me to not separate from you today. I repent from any destructive patterns, behaviors, thoughts, or processes. I surrender my heart to you today, in Jesus's name, Amen.

Just like it feels good to have a clean house, it also feels good to have a clean soul. And it will help us remain strong in the places that cause us to feel our weakest and most alone. In just a minute we will see a powerful lesson unfolding in the story of Moses as it connects to the wrongs that God can make right in our lives.

Just because we make decisions that don't reflect the character of God doesn't mean they have to define us for our entire lives. We may feel separated from God by our sin, but we are not—because of the grace of Jesus.

And even though Moses's story is before the cross, there is grace to be found in his story. In ours too.

Surrounded and Separated

We see quite a few contrasts between Jesus and Moses when we study their stories closely. So far in our study of Moses, some of the similarities we've seen are:

- evidence of God's miraculous power at birth
- two birth parents who feared God more than man
- a childhood of preparation (Moses in the palace, Jesus in the synagogue)

And we are about to see one very painful common denominator—being rejected and threatened by their people:

> When he went out the next day, behold, two Hebrews were struggling together. And he said to the man in the wrong, "Why do you strike your companion?" He answered, "Who made you a prince and a judge over us? Do you mean to kill me as you killed the Egyptian?" Then Moses was afraid, and thought, "Surely the thing is known."
>
> When Pharaoh heard of it, he sought to kill Moses.
>
> Exodus 2:13–15

While Moses's rejection from the Hebrews is similar to Jesus's rejection from the Jews, there is a major difference. Moses was responsible for his actions, while Jesus suffered because of the choices of another. Jesus was arrested by the temple officers because of the duplicity of one of His disciples, although

Jesus Himself knew all along what Judas would do (Matthew 26:47–50).

Still, they both experienced separation from people they once called friends.

Jesus and Moses both became surrounded by people who hated them and became separated from people who loved them. Different circumstances but same outcome: separation.

And this is where I exhale and begin to invite you into a hard conversation.

There are times in our lives when transition brings us to a place of separation that will appear completely unfair. And yes, like my brother and Moses, our own decisions can lead us to this place.

But here's the thing. While I don't think God was pleased with the decision Moses made to kill the Egyptian, the reality is, Moses couldn't stay with those people, his own adopted family.

His assignment from God was beyond the walls of Pharaoh's palace.

Sometimes when we become separated from someone or something, it might become what we need to get to the next place in our life. But other times, like with my brother, it destroys us more. I present both of those options today because they are just that, options.

We have to own our part in this process with God.

So as you're thinking about the places where you are experiencing a transition season of separation, remember this: whether we made the decisions that got us to this place or it was completely unfair, it's here. And God will use this to show us that He is what we need in this season the most. Not our mom, our sister, our BFF, or anyone else in our current community.

And here's the best news:

God's grace, forgiveness, and mercy for
resetting our new twenty-fours is something
beyond our human comprehension.

I know sometimes in a season of transition it feels like we're never going to break the cycles we are in. The loneliness of a season of separation can bring out less than the best in us. But each day is a new twenty-four. As the sun rises, God's mercy meets us again.

It's another day, another moment, and another opportunity to receive His forgiveness.

What the enemy of our souls delights over,
God destroys in the blink of an eye with His
forgiveness. What we confess, He can bless.

We will learn later on in Moses's story that at the right time, God will bring the right people into our lives to help us get to that next space in our lives. But until we fully embrace that God is what we need the most, it's going to be hard to move on.

As we close out this chapter, here are three practical ways to try this right now.

Three Ways to Help You See God Is What You Need, Today

1. Turn your phone on silent for two hours. Go about your day but do not look at that phone. Every time you feel lonely or isolated, instead of reaching for your phone, pray this: "*God, help me be aware of You right here, right now.*"

2. Make a list of the people this season of your life has caused you to separate from, for whatever reason

(death, conflict, a move, etc.). Describe why it's so hard not to see those people and what they did in your life. Ex: My mom was always there for me on hard days but now she's not.

3. Identify the character traits these people had that you are missing in your life, and try to find them in God by looking up verses about His character. Ex: My mom was always there on a hard day, and I wish I could call her, but I know the Bible says in 1 Peter 5:7 that I can cast my cares on Jesus because He is there.

5

Turning Tassels

We stood in the warm Charlotte late-spring sun with our hunter green caps and gowns with yellow-gold tassels that held a '99 pendant. The pomp and circumstance music began, and we walked our way onto the dew-dipped grass at the Independence High School football stadium.

The guest commencement speaker arose at the appropriate time. She told a few jokes about parents and their aging process through the teenage years. She reminded us of the good and the hard about high school. And she closed by saying something we've all heard a dozen commencement speakers say: "Today is the first day of the rest of your life. Live it well. It goes by fast."

And then, they told us to take our tassels and move them from the right to the left, a new season started now.

Graduation.

It's such a clear transition season of separation in life.

You begin in one place, kindergarten, and if all goes pretty well, you end on the other side, your high school graduation day. In a graduation ceremony, the turning of the tassel from right to left symbolizes one season is ending and a new one is beginning.

But in real life, there are no tassels to turn when the next season is coming. And this new now, the place we are between here and there, lasts a lot longer than a graduation ceremony. And don't you wish starting a new season was as simple as turning a tassel from right to left?

There are lots of life transitions of separation we can prepare for, like graduations or living on your own, getting married, starting your first job, having a baby, moving a family to a new city, or becoming an empty nester. These places we are somewhat warned about, and most of the time we see them coming.

But many transitions do not come with a forewarning.

Regardless of the way a transition comes, you can become a person of grace, dignity, honor, and godliness no matter what tassels get turned in your life. There's a shaping of your character that is happening in each place of transition. The growth you experience today, right now, will eventually reflect in your next season.

Today is the first day of the rest of your life. It goes by fast. Those are words we need to remember. Recognizing the need to value each day with this same perspective can make transitions feel like they have meaning and purpose.

We're not just wandering alone. God is showing us He's what we need and that He is with us, in the highs and the lows. But it's up to us to decide we're going to see Him.

Let's see how this played out in Moses's life.

Fleeing and Changing

Where we last left Moses, he had killed the Egyptian and had been found out. Shortly after that, Pharaoh got word of what happened, and Moses had one choice to keep his life: flee.

When Pharaoh heard of it, he sought to kill Moses. But Moses fled from Pharaoh and stayed in the land of Midian. And he sat down by a well.

Exodus 2:15

Pharaoh's anger toward Moses was not so much to redeem the death of the Egyptian Moses had killed, but rather it was the discovery that this child he had allowed to grow up in his own palace had become a traitor.

Pharaoh is mad and rightly so. So, Moses decides that he will flee from Egypt to a place called Midian.

This was a long and lonely journey for Moses. He had a lot of time to think about the choices he had made and the fact that the life he had always known would be no more. This permanent separation from being a prince in the palace was a necessary part of his process.

But as Moses makes his way into Midian, he is still dressed like an Egyptian and he still has the schooling and skills of an Egyptian. After all, there was no Target for him to pop into and buy a wardrobe change on his way out of Egypt. And there wasn't a YouTube channel to help him "deconstruct" from being an Egyptian.

What a picture this is for us.

As we enter seasons of separation, we often carry things from the previous season with us. We look, talk, and act the same, but everything is different, and a lot of the time people in our lives change too. This is where loneliness can start to write the story of looking back on what was.

And so, we do the only things we know how to do, the old things.

For some of us, this can be the coping mechanisms I referenced in the last chapter, or the ways we check out from reality. For others, it could be thinking that we must replicate what the last season brought us. So we look for the same job, the same type of people . . . the same "clothes," but it's the wrong attire and attitude.

Are you hoping I'm about to tell you that it's time to throw all your clothes away and go buy new ones?

I am not. IN FACT.

Would you believe me if I told you that in my own season of separation, God convicted me so deeply about how many new clothes I was buying, "to cope"? I wanted so badly to hurry up and get to the next season, I took on the secular stance of *dressing for the life you want.*

Listen, there's nothing wrong with a new outfit. Just don't believe the lie that somehow with what you wear outwardly you can rush what God is doing inwardly.

> What God is doing inwardly
> cannot always be displayed outwardly.

And sometimes this can take years. The life of Moses can be divided up almost perfectly into three sections of forty years (40, 80, and 120). Where we've arrived with Moses at this point, he is forty years old. And what we're about to see happen in Moses was that this process of separation for him would take around another forty years.

Y'all, YEARS.

Chances are, we don't all have forty years. And because of the lessons we are learning from Moses, it doesn't have to take us years to learn what each transition season has to teach us.

But, it's time to do some more work.

Sit Down

I think I realized how different my life was going to be the first time we were able to Zoom with the three boys we are adopting.

Having raised three girls, I've quickly seen how different boys and girls can be, especially their energy levels.

As the meeting loaded on my computer screen, I saw these three little heads bobbing around, smiling and giggling while jumping up and jumping down. They were flying their Spiderman action figures across the table, and the social worker conducting the meeting gave me this humorous look of *do you really know what you're getting into?*

He frequently told the boys to sit down, and they would, for a minute.

Do we know what we're getting into? Absolutely not. Which is the theme of our lives. When my husband and I got married at nineteen, we had no idea what we were getting into. When we started our company, we had no idea what we were doing. When we bought our farm eight years ago, we had no clue what we were doing. And most days, we still don't.

But obviously, adoption isn't something you can just jump into blindly. We've spent years now preparing for this, learning from others, and asking ourselves some really hard questions about what it will mean to bring these three boys into our lives and us into theirs. Still, I don't think we will really know what this is going to be like until they are home.

But watching those lively boys jump around on a Zoom meeting had my husband laughing at the number of times we will potentially say, "Sit down."

Girls get fidgety too, but I'm suspecting every boy-momma is nodding her head while reading this, saying, "Yep, get ready." Boys are just wired differently, so I'm learning.

This adoption has been a long season of separation that has been hard and complicated. The boys are experiencing one process of separation, and we are too. In transition places like this, our souls can look a little like the activity on that Zoom meeting. Bouncing from this place to the next and not really wanting to sit down in this space we are at, today. And I picture God saying, "Sit down. Just sit down."

I realize the majority of you reading this are not in the process of adoption. But think for a minute about where you are and where you've been. How has a transition season of separation made your brain feel like you are bouncing from here to there? Are you resisting "sitting" with this place in your life?

As Moses arrived in Midian, he did this: "And he sat down by a well" (Exodus 2:15).

Weary, tired, lonely, and heartbroken Moses arrives in the place he will spend the next part of his life discovering God may not be all he wants, but all he needs. The place he sits first? A well. This is such a vital picture of what's happening in Moses's life at this point.

Throughout the Bible, we can see examples of wells being a transition point in someone's story. A few of my favorites are:

- The angel finding Hagar at the well (Genesis 16)
- Jacob arriving in Harran and meeting Rachel at the well (Genesis 29)
- The Samaritan woman meeting Jesus at the well (John 4)

Some Bible scholars believe that wells in the Bible symbolize a place of access and supply. Others believe they represent a place of community, since the well was a gathering place. But Moses, as he arrives at this well, needs all three: access, supply, and people.

He has become separated from the life he knew for forty years, and there are tangible things he needs and wants. But the greatest thing his soul needs? God's presence.

God's presence is the greatest thing you and I need in any season we are in.

Read with me Exodus 2:15-16 so that you can see what I saw when I was studying this:

> When Pharaoh heard of it, he sought to kill Moses. But Moses fled from Pharaoh and stayed in the land of Midian. And he sat down by a well. Now the priest of Midian had seven daughters, and they came and drew water and filled the troughs to water their father's flock.

This is powerful. Moses sits down by the well in verse fifteen, and then in verse sixteen, we see the beginning of the things he needs (a wife, community, purpose, etc.) start to enter into his life, right there at the well.

But we can't have verse sixteen without verse fifteen. The significance of these two verses and the events they contain—coming to the well and sitting down—are such a powerful picture of Moses's process with God.

He had been running, hiding, and now it was time to stop.

If we go back to the original Hebrew language of verse fifteen, the word used for "sat down" was *yashab*, which means to sit, remain, dwell. Biblical scholars tell us that the word *yashab* is closely connected to the presence of God. Moses wasn't in a rush to leave this place; God was meeting him there.

We know it's essential at times in our lives to sit down. We see the significance in the Scriptures of coming to the well. But are we willing to sit with God at our well until we are able to see He is truly what we need the most?

The *until* is where a lot of us part ways with God, because it just gets too hard and we are impatient humans. And it's where those destructive decisions (sin) enter into our lives. The temptation to rush through this place with God is all around.

To overcome the loneliness and feelings of being lost, we're going to have to sit down and seek Him. We have to stop trying to hide and run. We can look at the season we're leaving and say, *It's time for me to go sit at my well.* And then we stay at the well as long as we need to so that we can start to look ahead at what God is doing.

But, if we don't grasp what this means to us personally to *sit down at the well*, we tend to walk right into that next season trying to wear those "old clothes," missing the new thing God wants to do in our lives.

And then in the next season, we can become the same emotional and spiritual mess, again.

Your transition season of separation holds a defining moment of needing to *sit down at your well.* It's easy to say, "God is all I need and want." But that is not an easy statement to live out.

Especially if our choices have led us into this transition season of separation—just like Moses's choice led him to Midian.

When we decide we're going to sit down at the well, it won't be a magical place where everything suddenly becomes right in our lives. But it is the place we clearly see the One who makes all things right in our souls—Jesus.

And I don't know about you, but the more I see Jesus, the more I want to sit with Him.

Jesus is a comforter, but He is also a challenger.

There are days when I need the presence of Jesus like I did in my brother's ICU room. And then there are days when I need the presence of Jesus to remind me, "Hey, we've got some work to do today, come sit down."

When I think about this place with God, I think of these two verses:

> Therefore let everyone who is godly
> offer prayer to you at a time when you may be found;

surely in the rush of great waters,
they shall not reach him.
You are a hiding place for me;
you preserve me from trouble;
you surround me with shouts of deliverance. *Selah*

Psalm 32:6–7

When we have work to do with God, there is hope like no other that meets us there. Our well is not only a sanctifying place, but it's also a saving place. It's a place of provision and protection, where the goodness of God also meets the grace of God.

And we should be so expectant, no matter what season we are in, to come to our well.

This is your well, your encounter. Jesus meets us all in different ways. But it's always for the same outcome: so that we will experience how He is what we need.

If this concept of coming to your well is still feeling a little fuzzy in your mind, let's spend the last part of this chapter figuring out what this might look like for you.

Meeting With the CEO of Your Life

Earlier we talked about God being the CEO of your life. What if you thought about coming to your well the same way you would with having a meeting with a corporate professional CEO?

Most CEOs don't have the capacity to work in a last-minute meeting with anyone. But God, He's just that good, because He does. He's already at your well, ready to meet with you. So time is not a constraint with Him.

But if you were going to have an intentional meeting with a CEO, do you agree you might do some things to prepare? Here are a few things you could do to prepare to meet with God, today, at your well.

1. Keep a positive perspective about the outcome of this encounter with God. Remember God doesn't invite us to our well for a shaming session. This is a place of change and challenge.

2. Write down everything you need wisdom from God about during this transition space in your life. Try not to think ahead into the future, just where you are today.

3. Bring your ideas, dreams, and hopes to your well, your meeting place with God. But be willing to lay them all down in surrender.

4. Have a notebook ready to write down anything you sense the Lord revealing to you. Be ready to write down thoughts that pop up, questions that stir, verses He brings to your mind, and convictions or challenges you begin to see.

5. Don't be afraid to ask God for big things at your well. Our God is a miracle-working God.

6. Decide to begin and end this time with God in worship. Be prepared to have a few songs ready to play.

You can do this. Come to your well. Meet with God. Seek His wisdom and find His ways for this season of your life.

6

You Are Not Really "That Thing"

I thought I would forever be known as the girl who got pregnant at nineteen before she was married. And to a very small amount of people, maybe I still am.

I used to frequently share my story publicly of Church wounds from that season and the way those wounds propelled me to where I am today. That story and that process served me and the Church well for a season.

But over time, I began to sense it was time to stop letting that be the anchor of who I was as a Bible teacher and communicator. While I was *sitting at my own well*, God revealed to me that was how I started, but that's not who I was anymore. It was time to separate from "that thing" of being known as the girl who got pregnant before she was married and was hurt by her church.

This meant changing a lot of things and separating myself from people who would always look at me with pity because of the decisions I had made as a teenager. I stopped agreeing to do interviews that were solely based on that part of my story. I stopped processing it through my writing. And very rarely did I ever use it as an example when I was teaching at events.

It doesn't mean I don't still deeply relate to people who send me their Church-hurt stories or care for people in similar situations. Just a few weeks ago, a pastor (with my permission) had given my phone number to a mom in his church who had just found out her teen daughter was pregnant. I talked to her for a few minutes and encouraged her about the season she was in, but not much else came from that conversation. It's not that I don't want people to hear my story anymore, but it became a place I needed to separate from in order to grow.

What is "that thing" in your life you just don't feel like you can separate from? Maybe it's a label, identity, or connection you just don't want anymore.

A separation transition season is a perfect place to part ways with "that thing." But it's going to require some intentional effort. Like having conversations with people who may look down on you a certain way. You may need to ask them to see you in a new way. Or maybe it's removing yourself from a group of people "that thing" is negatively associated with.

This takes time, and I wish we could somehow hurry up the process of separating our identity from something that no longer serves us well. Thankfully we're learning from Moses, and we know his process at this point in his life took forty years.

He knew he couldn't and didn't want to be an Egyptian anymore, but I'm assuming he also didn't want the reputation of a murderer. Not only was there a separation of his life as he sat down at the well, he also began a separation of his false identity.

After Moses arrived in Midian, he sat down at the well, but he was still being judged for being an Egyptian because of how he looked. I'm sure there were some whispers from the community members who also were gathering at the well. Things like, "Ugh, what is that Egyptian doing here?"

But there was a priest in Midian who had seven daughters. On the exact day Moses was sitting at the well, they also arrived at the well to water their father's flock. But some other shepherds showed up and were being rude to these women, pushing them away.

Moses is still Moses, willing to fight for injustice. This time, though, he fought the right way.

> The shepherds came and drove them away, but Moses stood up and saved them, and watered their flock.
>
> Exodus 2:17

I wonder if we're ever afraid to sit at the well with Jesus because He might squash out those things we believe make us "us."

For example, I know someone who has told me countless times they cannot drink alcohol without becoming drunk because they don't like who they are when they are sober. I know other people who believe if they don't use profanity when they talk, no one will listen. And I even know someone who won't stop having an affair because she thinks if she does, she will never have moments of happiness again.

The thing is, all those people I know love Jesus. They are all in a transition season of separation. They just haven't been able to fully sit at the well with Jesus so that He can become what they need *and* want.

And so, getting to that next season of their lives feels almost impossible but also incredibly unexciting.

Moses is teaching us we can separate from sin and still be significant, incredible people in our generations. Moses became a hero to those women that day. And because of his heroic act, Moses was about to be blessed with something he wanted: a wife.

Seven Possible Brides

These seven daughters rushed home from the well to tell their father the excitement of the day. It's interesting to note their father has two different names in Scripture: Reuel (Exodus 2:18) and Jethro (Exodus 3:1). Why? I have no clue. I just wanted you to be aware as you study this on your own, so it doesn't get too confusing.

Their father rewards Moses by giving him one of his daughters, Zipporah, as his wife.

> And Moses was content to dwell with the man,
> and he gave Moses his daughter Zipporah.
>
> Exodus 2:21

The next part is something I don't want us to miss. Not only does Moses get married and begin to build a new life, but he also has a son, and look what the Scriptures tell us about this baby:

> She gave birth to a son, and he called his name Gershom, for
> he said, "I have been a sojourner in a foreign land."
>
> Exodus 2:22

Ger means "foreigner, stranger," and *sham* means "there." Moses was a stranger there—a sojourner.

Most names in the Bible hold significant meanings. Another example I love is when Jacob renamed his son from Ben-oni, which meant "son of my sorrow," to Benjamin, which meant "son of my favor" (Genesis 35:18).

If you studied Ruth with me in the Bible study *A Woman Who Doesn't Quit*, this may sound familiar. That word, *sojourn*, is so significant because it means "temporary stay."

At this point, we are seeing some huge growth in Moses. Not only is his life turning around from that huge mistake he made, but he realizes, *I'm just a stranger passing through.* Moses hasn't quite found his place, but he is on his way.

I want us to hold on to this, because there is so much truth and hope packed into that one word *sojourn*. A transition is a temporary place.

> **Being willing to accept the temporary places of separation helps us build a permanent future filled with God's promises for our lives.**

Moses left Egypt; his change of residency was permanent. But those things that led up to this transition in his life were temporary. They didn't define him forever.

Yesterday I was talking to a friend who is also a speaker. She had recommended me to speak at an event, and the event coordinator said, "Oh yes, I've heard of her. The Bible-teacher-farm girl."

And I realized, God has grown me from the girl who got pregnant before she was married. The farm girl part makes me laugh, because I still have a hard time calling myself that. I mean, I fed the chickens this morning in my pajamas because these early morning chores often must get done before I have time to get dressed for the day. Still trying to nail down that Bible-teacher-farm-girl life.

But still, growth is growth.

Moses's title also changed. But maybe not in the way he had hoped. In fact, some might have looked at this title as a downgrade, because he went from son of a princess to shepherd in a field.

Moses didn't know this, but this new title would also be temporary. Very soon (well, another forty years "soon") he would go from being demoted as prince to becoming a deliverer to God's people.

And that's a title anyone would also be . . . COMPLETELY FREAKED OUT BY.

When a Complicated Separation Is Filled with Simple Tasks

I have so many favorite parts of the story of Moses. And heads up, there is no possible way we will cover all of the events of Moses's life in this book. But I think if I had to choose the one moment I identify with the most, it's this one we are about to study.

> And God heard their groaning, and God remembered his covenant with Abraham, with Isaac, and with Jacob. God saw the people of Israel—and God knew.
>
> Exodus 2:24-25

While Moses had slipped off into this new life, not much had changed in Egypt. Except for the death of Pharaoh. As I studied this, some scholars do believe this Pharaoh who died was the same Pharaoh who sought to kill Moses (his grandfather). The Israelites (Hebrews) were still enslaved by the Egyptians, and they were crying out to God for help.

There are four powerful words in the verses above we need to pay attention to.

1. God heard
2. God remembered
3. God saw (or considered)
4. God knew (was concerned)

While Moses was living out his transition season of separation, God was working in ways Moses knew nothing about. And we need to keep this reminder for the days when it seems like God is doing nothing in our lives.

> When we sit at our wells, He hears, He remembers, He sees, and He knows.

But God's timing is not explainable with human logic.

Because, for another forty years, Moses would live his life in the desert, raising his family and shepherding sheep. Living a fairly simple life.

This could sound boring compared to the excitement of the first forty years of his life. In fact, it could seem like this very simple season Moses was living in was not the actual preparation he needed for the season ahead.

> Never underestimate the strength that today's simple tasks can give you when God knows complicated is just ahead.

Often in a transition season of separation, it can feel as though we are doing nothing important. But these mundane days hold something we need.

First, these simple places offer more time at the well. When we're not in a crisis, or the newness of a season ending has worn off, the well can be one of the last places we want to be. But as you are waiting for God to show you who and what is next, learning to become whole with just you and Him is a gift.

Second, these simple places allow a transition season of separation to become a season of preparation. Even when we don't know what's next or what's ahead, just like Moses, tending sheep day after day . . . there are lessons to be learned.

Even the simple places of life can become days we experience the serenity of God. While I don't enjoy mundane farm chores like scooping manure or grooming a mini horse that likes to bite me, these simple tasks each day give me some space to breathe and experience God's presence outside.

God was hearing, remembering, seeing, and knowing what the Israelites needed. And then one day, God looked upon a field and saw this faithful shepherd who sat at a well, turned his life around, and lived out the simplicity of the season at hand. And God said, "Alright, it's time." And suddenly a bush was on fire, and life as Moses knew it was about to change.

The Fiery Non-Burning Bush

> Now Moses was keeping the flock of his father-in-law, Jethro, the priest of Midian, and he led his flock to the west side of the wilderness and came to Horeb, the mountain of God. And the angel of the LORD appeared to him in a flame of fire out of the midst of a bush. He looked, and behold, the bush was burning, yet it was not consumed.
>
> Exodus 3:1–2

This is one of the most famous scenes in Scripture. Moses was tending his sheep and then suddenly a bush is on fire, but it's not actually burning. For forty years Moses has had his sandals in this dirt of this desert. He has never seen or experienced anything like this. But here's something interesting: the Hebrew word for "desert" is *midbar*, which comes from the word *dabar*, which can mean "to speak."

A transition season of separation can feel very much like we are in our own desert. We can feel like God just dropped us in this really hot and dry place in our lives and we can feel forgotten. But the ways that God has spoken to me personally in these seasons of separation have become some of my most sacred places.

Isaiah 55:8 reminds us, "For my thoughts are not your thoughts, neither are your ways my ways, declares the LORD."

So, what often looks like isolation to us can really be an invitation into a deeper place with Him. And we're about to see this desert become a very vital place for Moses too.

Moses decides to take a closer look at this fiery bush, and he realizes it is now calling his name:

> When the LORD saw that he turned aside to see, God called to him out of the bush, "Moses, Moses!" And he said, "Here I am."
>
> Exodus 3:4

At this point, Moses has no idea this is God. And just to dig a little deeper into Exodus 3:4, we notice how God repeats Moses's name twice: "Moses, Moses!"

There is an urgency expressed in God's way of calling out to Moses. And there is also an urgency in how God calls out to you today.

It's important for us to understand that the bush was not God. But it was the way God chose to get the attention of Moses. A bush on fire was most likely something Moses had seen before. But a bush on fire that wasn't burning up was unusual.

I wonder how many times God tries to use ordinary things to get our attention and we completely miss them. If we would just look a little closer at the ordinary, we might see God doing something miraculous we can't explain.

When God Starts to Call You Out of Separation

We've worked through two seasons of transition so far: development and separation. And I wish we were all at the same point

Moses is in his process: being called out of separation. Moses is getting ready to be called into the next transition season of his life, a transition season of cultivation, which we'll study next.

We are always in some place of transition. And my hope is that as we start to see how God is actively moving in our lives, we will stop resisting the process of transition. We can walk through these places of our lives confident that while we may feel lost or alone, God is doing things behind the scenes we just don't know about yet.

For some of us, God is also going to call us out of the place of separation very quickly. But for others, we are just entering this transition place in our lives. And our souls may already be resisting staying here much longer.

May we take the lessons Moses has taught us in this section of the book and believe that if God could do this for Moses, He can do this for us. We've discovered how in a transition season of separation God is what we need the most, and eventually He will become what we want the most. We figured out how to sit at our wells. We've seen how mistakes can separate us for a season, but they don't have to define us for the rest of our lives. And we've learned how not to resist the simple places of a transition season of separation because they often become the most significant places God speaks to us.

If you don't feel like your transition season of separation is ending, you may have to come back and read this last page of this section later on in your life. But the promise to hold on to in all these places of transition is that it does eventually change over to the next season.

Moses was in this desert for forty years.

I don't think it's going to take you that long. But I know if you will keep sitting at your well, keep looking for God in the ordinary, and keep listening in expectation for His voice . . . He will call you into the next place of your life.

How will you know you're being called out of separation?

I wish I could tell you exactly what this will look like for you, but I don't know. However, if we look at Moses, we see in the midst of the ordinary, God shows up. So maybe don't look for a burning bush, but look for things God uses to get your attention. And ask the Lord to make you aware.

Second, the door of *what's next* may not swing open, but it will crack open. You'll start to see little glimmers of light coming into those once-dark places of your soul. And lastly, I really believe you'll want and desire to be at your well more than anywhere else in your life. The well is the best place to hear God calling you by name, just like He did with Moses. You may feel like you're missing it, but as you build consistency with God, you will look back eventually and say, "I see it now."

Alright, friend. High fives for making it halfway through this book. We've still got more work to do, but I think you're gonna love this next section. It's my favorite type of transition: cultivation. And we will study together what happens to Moses after he hears God call his name. It's about to get a little wild for Moses.

In-Between-Seasons
Mini Bible Study

Read Exodus 3

What was the name of the mountain where Moses was tending his sheep (Exodus 3:1)?

Study note: It's important to note that this mountain will also be referred to as Mt. Sinai, and we will see Moses return to this place.

In Exodus 3:6, who does God say He was?

Why do you think Moses hid his face from God?

In Exodus 3:8, where does God say He's going to take the Israelites?

    a. To the land of good and evil

    b. To the land flowing with milk and honey

    c. To the land of fruit and vegetables

Study note: Remember, the official name for this land is Canaan.

List out all of the "I Am" statements from Exodus 3:13–15.

Below is a chart to help you define Moses's life stages more clearly. Look up each of the verses and write them out in the box.

Three Stages of Moses's Life

LOCATION	AGE	WRITE OUT VERSES
Egypt	0–40	Exodus 2:11 Acts 7:23
Midian	41–80	Exodus 2:15 Acts 7:29–30

LOCATION	AGE	WRITE OUT VERSES
The wilderness	81–120	Deuteronomy 31:2 Numbers 14:33–34

Were there any keywords, verses, or themes that stood out to you in Exodus 3? List them below—and bonus points for looking up the original meaning of those keywords.

_____

_____

_____

_____

_____

CULTIVATION

7

Finding a *Holy Now*

About fifteen years ago, I was frustrated with the way it seemed women studied the Bible in my community. The in-person Bible studies I had been part of felt perfection-driven and gossipy.

Once, during prayer time in my study group, someone expressed frustration about another member of the group. Apparently, this woman who wasn't there that day had complained to others about the study and then didn't show up consistently.

Someone else in the group replied to this gossip-disguised-as-a-prayer-request: "Well, maybe she should just start her own Bible study."

And at that moment, my heart began to flutter. Something about that statement was speaking to me. I wasn't yet brave enough to speak out in a group setting like that, but as I was driving home later, God met me on the highway in my car.

I remember praying, *"God, one day I'm gonna do that very thing, start my own Bible study, and it's not going to be like this."*

I felt like God high-fived me on that highway and something holy was birthed from my anger and frustration. You could say a seed was planted in me.

I never went back to that Bible study. I did start my own. And *eventually*, it turned into what I'm doing today.

That night was a moment of transition in my life. But it would take almost a decade of what I consider the longest season of cultivation in my life to see the fruit from that decision in the car.

In fact, I'm still in a season of cultivating this calling God revealed to me after the Bible study. There is so much I still have to learn. I definitely don't think I've arrived.

The third season we are going to discuss in this section of the book is a transition season of cultivation.

One of the meanings of the word *cultivation* is related to the preparation of land for the raising of crops. *Cultivate* is a very intentional word, and if this season isn't spent doing very intentional things, we can miss the growth this season offers.

> There is a difference between
> having intentions and being intentional.

And that is one of the greatest lessons we can learn during a transition season of cultivation: intentional > intentions.

We've all heard people say things like, "Oh, I had all the intentions to call you today, I just forgot!" Or, "I had the best intentions to work out today, but you know, I just got busy."

Intentions, if not followed through, can simply become an excuse.

Being intentional means we're going to do our best to make space, develop habits, research, or do whatever we need to do so that what needs to happen, happens. In this section of the book, my hope is that you will be challenged to replace intentions with being intentional and cultivate the new things God is doing in your life.

Differing Between Development and Cultivation

We finished learning about a transition season of separation in the last section of the book, and it's easy to see the difference between separation and cultivation.

But one of the questions you may have is how a season of cultivation differs from a season of development.

Development is recognizing the need to improve or expand on something you already have in your life (the seed) in the midst of transition. Development can also be the process of correcting, improving, or changing something.

Remember how we looked at our childhood and the ways we developed based on our life circumstances (such as my adaptability due to moving so many times)? We even identified some things that could have been developed in us that we needed to rethink. For example, Moses decided he no longer wanted to be an Egyptian even though he had spent his entire life being developed into one.

Rather than changing *existing* characteristics within us, a transition season of cultivation offers us *new* habits, perspectives, and preparation for the assignments God has for us now and into the next season.

This is a season that produces something, and to stick with the farming perspective, it's the fruit or crop that can come from the transition. But also, if we don't care for ourselves and this process, this season could yield what looks like weeds in our lives.

Some of you will thrive in this type of transition season! But if you are someone who struggles with change and learning new things, it may take time for you to feel excited about this season. It may be harder for you than anyone around you knows.

No matter which side of that spectrum you find yourself on, Moses has a lot to teach us. And I'm here with you, guiding us both through this process.

Here are some examples of the way life can lead you into a transition season of cultivation:

- A stay-at-home mom needs to enter or reenter the workforce. Things have changed since the last time she worked outside the home, and it feels like there's a whole new world out there she has to learn.
- The college graduate gets her first job based on her degree but needs to learn a whole new set of skills to actually do the job she's been hired to do. She wonders if her degree will help her at all.
- Someone retires from a career but doesn't just want to hang out at home all day. So they want to learn a new hobby or skill set to continue to feel purpose in life.
- Technology changes, and to keep up with our careers or advance in our careers, we have to learn the changes.
- The high school graduate isn't quite ready for college or a career, and so she spends a few months experiencing a variety of things like travel or different jobs.
- You are given a new role in life or in your career that you feel very unqualified for.
- You begin to realize that people, places, or things that worked well in one season no longer work in this place you are today. There's a feeling of being dissatisfied with where you are, and you realize you need to make significant changes in your life to experience peace again.

Does any of this feel familiar? If so, write down an example from your life that might show you are in a transition season of cultivation:

_____

_____

_____

Change, change, change is the theme of all transitions, but this type of change in this season has really tangible results. Your routine, schedule, and calendar are all ways cultivation can start to externally show. But also, what's happening behind the scenes of your life is even more important.

Before we see this played out in our lives, let's identify it in Moses's life.

When Normal Becomes a *Holy Now*

In chapter six, we left off with our study of Moses in what appeared to be a normal scene in a day in the life of Moses. He was tending his sheep, doing his job, minding his business, and suddenly he sees a bush that is on fire but not actually burning. As if that was not strange enough, the bush begins to speak and calls out Moses's name. Not once, but twice.

> When the Lord saw that he turned aside to see, God called to him out of the bush, "Moses, Moses!" And he said, "Here I am."
>
> Exodus 3:4

There is something significant about God calling Moses's name twice: it shows the authoritative, clear voice of God. We see this in a few other places in Scripture when God is calling someone into a special encounter with Him.

In Genesis 22:11 the angel of the LORD says Abraham's name twice, God called the prophet Samuel twice in 1 Samuel 3:10, and then He called Saul's name two times in Acts 9:4. Also, we see Jesus on the cross, crying out to God not once, but twice (Matthew 27:46).

When God calls Moses's name twice, he answers, "Here I am." His response seems so calm, but it traces back to the Hebrew word *hineni*. This word is basically a declaration from a person to the one they are serving or of a student to a teacher. It's not the same as when our teachers would do a roll call in class to confirm we were there. It's more like when the teacher calls out for someone to read in class and a student raises their hand and says, "I will!"

When we see this phrase used in Scripture, we see the speaker being in a place of availability for God to use however He wants. Like Moses, in a transition season of cultivation, this is one of the most pure and humble things we can say to God.

"Here I am."

It would be nice if God would do a call out of assignments for those of us in transition, right?

"Who wants this?"

"OK, what about this one?"

"Any takers on the next option?"

But part of cultivation means we learn to accept *whatever* assignment God gives. Moses certainly didn't ask for the assignment to come, but he did make himself available.

> Is it risky to tell God we're available?
> For us, yes. But never for God.

Things continue to get really real with Moses and God:

> Then he said, "Do not come near; take your sandals off your feet,
> for the place on which you are standing is holy ground." And he
> said, "I am the God of your father, the God of Abraham, the God
> of Isaac, and the God of Jacob." And Moses hid his face, for he
> was afraid to look at God.
>
> Exodus 3:5–6

As God speaks, He tells Moses there is a boundary and con-
dition with this encounter: 1) Moses is not to come any closer.
2) He needs to take off his sandals. God is showing Moses that
in the midst of this seemingly ordinary day, something unusual
is happening, and it requires a different response.

After those two things are defined, then God reveals who
He is.

I wish the text told us if Moses immediately took off his shoes
or if it took a second for it all to sink in. The end of verse six tells
us that Moses hid his face in fear of God, so we know Moses took
this encounter seriously.

But I'm just trying to get in Moses's head for a second, because this had to shake him. For something so unusual to happen in the midst of his very ordinary day is such a powerful
picture of the way God brings us into encounters with Him.

Sometimes we save our encounters with God for things like
a worship night at church, a conference, or even our Sunday
morning church service. We think it's these spotlight places
where God's presence seems to manifest in ways we can't explain. And there is something very holy and powerful about
gathering corporately with other believers and cultivating the
presence of God, together.

But I want to introduce you to something I've been trying to
experience daily in my life. It's called a *holy now.*

These moments cannot be perfectly defined in a paragraph in a book, because the way God brings us into an encounter with Him is unique to each of us. So I'm cautious not to attempt to put God into any type of box or formula, because He often works in ways (like a burning bush) we simply cannot explain.

This concept of a *holy now* has changed the way I intentionally engage with God every day. I believe it will for you too.

Recognizing Your *Holy Nows*

A *holy now* can be the initial moment that propels us into a transition in our lives. It's a sacred place where God steps in to our common and reveals Himself in an uncommon way. These encounters are not to scare us, shame us, or guilt-trip us into doing something for God.

Sometimes these *holy nows* lead to big moments of cultivation transition in our lives, like this moment we are studying with Moses. It can be a clear moment where we are called from one thing to the next.

What happens during a *holy now* can become either a place of growth or a place of regression in our lives.

That night, in the car, God met me in the midst of a very ordinary evening, driving down a highway after a frustrating Bible study. It was a *holy now* in my life, when I knew I was having an encounter with God. It was a space on my timeline where God would begin to reveal a future assignment for me.

But I wonder how many smaller *holy nows* with God we miss because we are so distracted and disengaged from His presence?

Like those moments we brush off when we feel a prompting to pray over something in our lives. But we are just too busy to stop, and we think, *Oh, I'll pray about that later*. Later never comes, and we lose a *holy now* opportunity with God.

Or what if you see some type of wrong in this world and think, *It shouldn't be this way*, and God is high-fiving you and wants YOU to be the one to do something about it?

But if we shrug off these moments of stirring in us as things that just bother us, we may never take the steps to do anything. Doing nothing can make us miss the cultivation of something new God is doing, right in front of us.

I do believe sometimes God will allow us to experience something drastic like a burning bush to get our attention. But I also believe God has encounters with us in really simple ways. *Holy nows* surround us all day long. But we aren't always willing to recognize them as that. Sometimes we blow them off as coincidences.

We have to stop thinking about life with God as one big coincidence. God is a very intentional God who always follows through with His intentions. When God leads us into a *holy now*, there is great intention in it.

We don't need to over-spiritualize this process of identifying a *holy now*. The other day, I accidentally called someone on my phone and there was nothing to it, it was literally an accident. I felt like the person didn't believe me, and they actually texted me afterward and said, "Are you sure it was an accident?" I was like, YES. It was just an accident.

But running into someone who has been on your mind again and again? It could be a *holy now*. Or coming across a verse or theme in the Scriptures? Could be a *holy now*. Maybe multiple people keep sending you the same job posting; could be a *holy now*.

There can be incredible, spontaneous moments of *holy nows* too.

A few weeks ago, I was at the airport typing on my computer, and a man and his wife sat down next to me. The man noticed my Bible and asked me if I was a Christian. Turns out he was a preacher and was also working on a book. We even had some mutual acquaintances. We all exchanged numbers, and I've stayed in touch with these new friends. We are even going to partner in ministry with a few things.

It was a *holy now* I couldn't have ever expected.

If something comes across your path and you think it might be a *holy now*, cultivate it. Pray. Ask the Lord for wisdom and confirmation. Let it settle in you. If you wake up the next morning still thinking about it, press into it more.

What is something you can think of recently in your life that you may have thought was a coincidence but are now realizing might have been a *holy now*?

Our No-Coincidences God

Then the LORD said, "I have surely seen the affliction of my people who are in Egypt and have heard their cry because of their taskmasters. I know their sufferings."

Exodus 3:7

After forty years in the palace and forty years as a shepherd, it is possible Moses started to think his time on earth was winding down. He was settled into his life, and it was good.

But all this time while Moses was in this transition season of cultivation, his people, the Hebrews, were still suffering. I'm sure Moses had moments when he wondered if he could have done something different. Or maybe he still should. But then possibly he would remember his mistake, his separation, and the fear he held in his mind about what Pharaoh wanted to do to him because he killed the Egyptian.

But then, this *holy now* at the burning bush happens. It's where the plan of God begins to unfold. And it all starts with God identifying the injustice that was done to the Hebrews. In Exodus 3:7, God explains to Moses three specific things about what's going on:

1. God has seen the affliction of His people.
2. God has heard their cries.
3. God knows their sufferings.

God was so specific with His words. He didn't just sum up the Hebrew people's problems with something like *I know life has been really hard for them.* God showed us how into the details He really is.

However, if your transition season is taking a long time, it can be easy to believe God doesn't care about the details anymore.

I felt this way with our adoption the other night.

I know God has seen the affliction these three boys have faced. I know He has heard our cries for them to have a family. I know He sees the medical and basic needs of these children. But why is it when I pray and ask God to move this document or allow a certain phone call to happen, many, many days there seems to be zero movement happening?

You may have something in your life as well that you sensed God was leading you to do, but now it feels like one big frustration, because nothing seems to be happening.

It's unsatisfying, I know. But here's where I find comfort today.

The Hebrew people had continued to pray for forty years. They never stopped believing their God could rescue them. Surely they got frustrated. Surely they kept pleading their case to Him.

What they didn't know was God was working behind the scenes. Their prayers were cultivating a movement in their lives only God could do.

He had started the process of freedom for them, and something was going to be different, soon. Moses was in transition. He had been through his season of development and separation, and now he was entering into cultivating this calling from God.

This was the assignment God had placed on Moses's life since the day he was born.

But, did Moses's process cause delays? Possibly.

Have we caused delays in our process? Possibly.

The thing I have to keep reminding myself about places of transition is that sometimes the process doesn't involve just us. There are other people involved. Can others make mistakes that can cause delays? Yes. Have I ever made a mistake that has caused a delay in my process? Yes.

Whenever humans are involved in anything, there is a chance something is going to get messed up in the process. But here's the key: what feels like a delay to us, isn't to God. I find some resolve in my soul by reminding myself of the words we see from Job:

> "I know that you can do all things,
> and that no purpose of yours can be thwarted."

> ## Job 42:2

Read that verse as many times as you need to today.

The good news is, no matter how many *holy nows* we think we missed, parts of the process we messed up, or unexplainable delays in the fulfillment of God's purpose, there's no way His plan can be thwarted. God is kind, compassionate, and patient with our process. Nothing happening down here on earth catches Him off guard.

One of the best ways we can keep cultivating what God is doing right now in our lives is by identifying how a *holy now* can lead us to see what's right in our hands. And what we have in our hands is always enough to keep our process with God moving along. Let's learn how to do this in the next chapter.

8

The Fear of Not Knowing If It's God

I'm pretty sure I could have become a viral TikTok video last summer. And not because I mastered some trendy dance.

Kris saved up and bought something he had wanted for a long time: a boat. It's a decent boat, but like most everything else in our lives, it's a fixer-upper. Beyond the repairs that needed to be made, there was a learning curve to having a boat.

After taking the boat out a few times on one of our local lakes, Kris and I realized this needed to be a team effort to unload and reload the boat effectively and efficiently.

Which meant I had to learn how to do two things.

One: how to back the boat off the trailer into the lake so he could park the truck. I am proud to say, I can do that pretty well now.

But once that was mastered, it was time to learn part two: how to back the trailer up on the boat dock landing to load the boat after we were done for the day on the lake.

Here's what I need you to know in case you have never had the *pure delight* (please hear my sarcasm) of being at a boat dock on a busy day.

Some owners of boats can turn into small children throwing temper tantrums if they cannot load their boat into the lake in approximately 5.2 seconds after pulling up to the dock.

I have seen more yelling, honking, *choice* words, and fights at the lake boat dock than at any other "recreational" place in America.

Which is exactly the scene that unfolded the day it was time for me to learn how to back the trailer in. I nervously pulled the truck around and slowly backed it down the ramp, but then I got tripped up because I couldn't figure out the right way to turn the steering wheel. Kris was being really patient and tried to help me figure it out. But it was taking a few minutes.

And then, there he was.

The self-appointed CEO of Boat Dock Central in his red truck, with his red face and his rude words. He started yelling all kinds of things at me, beeping his horn, and rallying up the guy next to him to do the same. The stress of the situation and the choice of his words was sending me over the edge.

I had my own choice words for him too.

So, I opened the truck door and started to walk over to deliver them to him, but thankfully the Holy Spirit told me to turn around. All I could think of was . . . *I just know someone caught all that on video, and if I go over there and let him have my words, I'm done.*

Can you see the headline on our local news website? "Woman goes viral on TikTok over outrage at local boat dock."

Well done, Holy Spirit, well done.

Kris finished backing the trailer in and loaded the boat. And there has never been a more silent car ride home than that one.

Oh, man.

That was a rough and unsuccessful way to learn how to do something new.

And unfortunately, we are living in this viral video world, where if you try something in public and it doesn't work and someone catches it on video, off it goes into the viral video world.

You've been there too.

Those moments where you trip, make a mistake, or do something out of character and think . . . *I really hope no one saw that.*

As we continue to work through this concept of being in a transition season of cultivation, we may have more fears than becoming a laughed-at viral video.

There are serious fears, like *how do I know when it's God telling me to do something? What if I want to attempt something new and no one thinks I can do it?* Or, *what if I don't want to do what God wants me to do in my next season?*

All of these fears and other wonderings in this season are normal and should be expected. But part of cultivation is being willing to do the work regardless of our confidence in it. Let's start with one of the biggest confidence busters—struggling to know if it's God leading you into a new thing.

Knowing When It's God

In the next few verses of Exodus 3:7-20, a lot unfolds. I wish we had time to study every bit of this together, but y'all, we're gonna have to do some speed dating through this story in certain sections, or this book will be 300,000 words. Sweet Brown said it first, "Ain't nobody got time for that."[1]

This section is where God reveals the plan for Moses to set his fellow people, the Israelites, free from Egypt. It's where God tells him, *Tag, you're it, Moses!* (Exodus 3:11-12). The plan was laid out; Moses would go back to Egypt and tell Pharaoh that God said it was time to let the Israelites go free.

God was very intentional with His instructions and His comforting words about this massive assignment. And while this could have been something God did on His own, God loves to partner with His people, as we see in this verse: "Working together with him, then, we appeal to you not to receive the grace of God in vain" (2 Corinthians 6:1).

God was very intentional with who He selected for this assignment. But after receiving God's assignment, fear begins to cultivate in Moses's mind. He thinks about all the things that could go wrong, and for a little bit, it seems like he's trying to talk God out of the plan.

> Then Moses answered, "But behold, they will not believe me or listen to my voice, for they will say, 'The LORD did not appear to you.'"
>
> Exodus 4:1

In the margin of my Bible next to this verse I wrote: *What if they don't believe me?* This is one of the questions our souls struggle with in the midst of a transition season of cultivation. It was certainly the question Moses was wrestling down.

But if Moses doubted while he was standing in front of God, how are you and I supposed to know if God is leading us into something or not?

It all comes down to three things: Truth (the Bible), the Holy Spirit, and faith.

We all come from different faith experiences and backgrounds. But I think most of us would agree, Truth is Truth. The God of Moses is the same God of today. And He is who He says He is, and His Word is absolute Truth. We may not like everything the Bible says, but that doesn't make it untrue.

Most of us would also agree on faith. We trust our lives to something we cannot see.

**We may not always have a lot of faith,
but we know our God can do a lot with a little.**

However, the Holy Spirit, and how He works in our lives, can divide a conversation with Christians quickly.

No matter how you have been taught or what you believe about the Holy Spirit, we can find Truth with this without getting into a huge theological debate.

Here are three verses I believe can help unify us on this:

John 17:17 says, "Sanctify them in the truth; your word is truth."

Hebrews 11:6 says, "And without faith it is impossible to please him, for whoever would draw near to God must believe that he exists and that he rewards those who seek him."

John 4:24 says, "God is spirit, and those who worship him must worship in spirit and truth."

I absolutely believe God, through the Holy Spirit, can and still does speak to us individually in a real and powerful way. It's why I knew to text my friend a few weeks ago and tell her I was praying for her despite not knowing any of her current circumstances. She was struggling, and the Holy Spirit prompted me to pray for her.

But it took all three of those things working together for me to know it was God.

1. I know the Bible tells us to pray for others. So that prompting aligned with Truth.
2. I believe in the power of the Holy Spirit; He is always prompting us toward a deeper experience of faith. He stretches us to take steps of obedience.

3. Faith is risky. I could've been wrong and texted my friend and she could've said, "Um, nothing is wrong today."

You've had things in your life happen that are undeniably God. And you've had things that have made you wonder *Is this God?*

I wish I could tell you the perfect formula for knowing when it's God. And I'll be honest, I think I only get it right about 75 percent of the time.

But we cannot expect to cultivate Truth, the Spirit, or faith in our lives if we are not actually doing anything.

In this season you may need to bump up your prayer time or Bible study time. You may need to do something very intentional like only listen to worship music or fast. You may need to take risks and invite someone new over. You may need to quit the job and start the classes for the degree.

I don't know what it is for you, but I know it's something. When we're in the space between here and there, it's not time to just hang out and binge-watch TV.

You will fight these places in your life, the ones that make us want to stay cozy in our pj's or in the same circle of friends. Because often when our souls feel conflicted, we want to do what feels comforting.

Cultivation should not always feel comfortable.
But it should always feel challenging.

So each day, may we take steps to cultivate Truth, the Holy Spirit, and faith more and more.

Which of those three things do you need to cultivate more of in your life today?

A. Truth

B. Spirit

C. Faith

What is something practical you can do right now to culti-vate that?

Three Lessons God Taught Moses about Cultivation

While you are in a season of cultivation you may have fears. And our teacher, Moses, definitely had a lot of fears and excuses. But as I was studying this next section in Exodus, I noticed there were three lessons God taught Moses about cultivation, and I think this will help us too. Here we go.

Lesson One: God's name offers all the credentials we'll need

As Moses wrestles with the "What if they don't believe me?" question, God volleys right back with another question:

> The LORD said to him, "What is that in your hand?" He said, "A staff."
>
> Exodus 4:2

Moses asks his question to gain confidence, and God knows the answer to the question He poses. So, He's not asking it for the sake of clarity on His part, He's asking it for the sake of the calling on Moses.

And I believe God poses a similar question to us today. Because as we are waiting on the next season to begin or feel lost in the transfer of one season to the next, we can start to believe we're not qualified to be anything other than what we've always been. This isn't true. God wants us to consider what we already have in our hands that He can use for His purposes.

And hopefully, God is cultivating in you right here, right now, a belief there can be more ahead for your life than what has already passed. You may have thought that job or organization was "it." You may have thought that relationship was everything.

And you may have thought the opportunity to do _____ had passed you by.

But God is as much here in this place of transition in your life as He is when life feels settled and figured out. So if God reveals it to you, God calls you to it, and you know it's God, tell your fear that God's name is enough.

Now, things are going to get just a little weird, OK? Hang with me.

Moses answers God's question, and then in Exodus 4:3–7 the staff becomes a snake, Moses's hand becomes leprous, and then both go back to their previous form. During this time in the history of God's people, God's prophets had the credentials of signs and wonders (Deuteronomy 13:1–3), so God gave Moses some signs and wonders.

But we do not have to wait for a sign or wonder to believe that the name of God is enough.

> **God doesn't need anyone to cosign for your assignment.**

And one of the greatest stances of humility we can cultivate during a season of transition is this belief.

God's name is enough.

You do not have to fight, push, or earn your way into your next season of assignments from God. He has picked you. It may take you some time to fully understand where He's leading you, but this place between here and there is the place to declare His name in your life.

So, what's in your hands today?

Write what you can identify here:

1.

2.

3.

Cultivate those things, relationships, and possibilities in the name of our God, and watch Him do what only He can do.

Lesson Two: God will ask you to do things you don't want to do

Well, if you've ever thought YOU were stubborn and hard for God to get His message across to, watch what happens to our guy Moses. You can feel the tension in this scene of the Scriptures. After God shows Moses these two signs (the staff turning into a snake, and the leprous hand), He then reveals the third one:

> "If they will not believe you," God said, "or listen to the first sign, they may believe the latter sign. If they will not believe even these two signs or listen to your voice, you shall take some water from the Nile and pour it on the dry ground, and the water that you shall take from the Nile will become blood on the dry ground."
>
> Exodus 4:8-9

I know . . . more weird stuff. Blood on the ground is gross.

What we need to pay attention to is the part that says "*or listen to your voice*" (v. 9). God is trying to pull out something in Moses: his voice.

This is where Moses *really* starts to resist this cultivating process with God. And honestly, the next few verses sound like a straight-up fight between Moses and God. Moses has more excuses in verse 10. He's not a good speaker, TBN didn't give him his own show . . . blah, blah, blah.

And God rolls back another verbal nudge in verse 11, reminding Moses that HE IS IN CHARGE HERE.

And then, Moses is out of objections and so . . . he quits this assignment.

But he said, "Oh, my Lord, please send someone else."

Exodus 4:13

I am trying not to laugh while I'm writing this, but I cannot help it. I can relate to this a *little too much*.

"Oh, Lord, please don't make me be kind to this sassy teenager you gave me. SEND HER DADDY."

"Oh, Lord, please don't make me go speak at a Girl Scout camp in the middle of nowhere. SEND MY FRIEND TIFFANY."

"Oh, Lord, please don't make me respond kindly to someone who sends me an email question that Google can clearly answer for them. SEND THEM AN ALEXA."

But then, I'm also this girl who watches airplanes fly across the sky and thinks of all the places I'd like God to allow me to go speak (like in HAWAII), praying that Isaiah 6:8 prayer, "*Here I am! Send me.*"

Oh man, conviction is falling all over me right now. Because we've all been there, right? We are 100 percent down for the fun God assignments. The ones that feel easy and we feel very much qualified to do. Possibly what we were doing in our last season.

But when God asks us to cultivate a new assignment that doesn't sound fun, like Moses, we're out. And maybe that's one of the reasons we feel stuck between seasons.

We're looking for fun, and God is looking for faithful.

What if one of the prayers we cultivated in our life during this season was this: *God, show me how I can be faithful to You, today.* But beyond that prayer, we actually need to do the things that God shows us to do.

What is something you sense God asking you to do that you don't want to?

Lesson Three: God will send the right people

Thankfully God doesn't give up on Moses. God's angry (Exodus 4:14), but He still knows Moses is the guy for this job. I'm so thankful that no matter how much we give up on God, He never gives up on us. His grace meets us again and again.

God is kind and offers Moses one more thing: someone to stand by his side and speak for him when he doesn't feel like he can.

> Then the anger of the LORD was kindled against Moses and he said, "Is there not Aaron, your brother, the Levite? I know that he can speak well. Behold, he is coming out to meet you, and when he sees you, he will be glad in his heart. You shall speak to him and put the words in his mouth, and I will be with your mouth and with his mouth and will teach you both what to do. He shall speak for you to the people, and he shall be your mouth, and you shall be as God to him."
>
> Exodus 4:14-16

Don't miss this. Notice how it says God is recommending Aaron for this role and then He says, "*Behold, he is coming out to meet you*" (v. 14). Aaron was already on his way.

I know you have battled feelings of isolation and loneliness as we've worked our way through this message. But take hold of this: God knows who you need, and they are on their way.

What's weird about writing a book about transition is I feel like I've battled all of these struggles recently. I have felt so much like Moses—unsure. I've had spiritual battles while writing before, but for this book, it's been really intense and really personal.

The only thing I've wanted is someone just to understand how I feel.

I called one of my friends the other day and just had a good cry session. I was ready to quit everything. She was gracious and kind and talked me off the ledge.

However, this morning, I woke up feeling like I was on that ledge again.

But just a few minutes ago that friend sent me a gift card to have lunch at one of my favorite writing places, and all she said was, "I believe in you."

Those four words carried me through this chapter you're reading right now. God knew what I needed, and He sent it, just when I was at the edge of that cliff.

Moses was at the edge of his cliff.

Maybe you are at the edge of yours. I wish I could tangibly be in your life today and say those four words to you: I believe in you. I do. I hope you know that.

But I also know sometimes we just need an actual person by our side. So as we close this out, if you're feeling on the edge, this prayer is for you:

God, thank You for this person on the other side of these words. Thank You that you love them and You have not given up on them. And while Your name is enough to confirm their assignments, God, sometimes we need an Aaron. So, Lord, I believe that person is on their way to meet this reader. Help my friend reading this to be open to whoever You might send their way and to trust them. Thanks for not giving up on us, and thanks for meeting us on the edges of life, just in time. Amen.

9

Plagues, Passover, and a Promise

It was the first time I had gotten brave enough to ride this horse without one of my horse-riding friends present. But Kris was on the tractor doing some work around the barn. Since he was close by, I knew if I needed help, he was there.

Finn, the horse, was skittish that afternoon, but that wasn't unusual. However, my gut was sending me two conflicting messages: 1) You need to push past your fear and get on this horse; he has to see that you mean business. 2) Something is wrong/off with him; don't get on him.

I went with message one. I saddled him up and walked him over to the mounting block so I could climb up to put my boot into the stirrup and swing myself over the saddle.

But before I could even sit down correctly on the saddle, Finn began to take off.

I pulled back on the reins and shouted the command, "Whoa!" but there was no stopping him.

And the rest felt like a slow-motion scene from a movie.

Kris quickly put the tractor into park. He ran toward me as my body was flinging backward off Finn. My leg was caught in the stirrup, and I was suddenly on the ground. Somehow my foot came out of the stirrup, and then Finn was above my head and I began to feel the stomping of his hooves all around and on me. Finn unintentionally kicked me a few times in his attempt to escape the situation, then bolted off across the pasture.

My chest felt like it was collapsing from the adrenaline, my leg was stinging with pain, and I looked at Kris in shock and said, "Why did he do that to me?"

And then, it was as if every suppressed emotion from the shock of falling began to burst out of me.

My body was bruised, my ankle sprained, but my heart was shattered. It had taken me months to get brave enough to attempt to ride Finn alone. My instincts were conflicted about whether to ride or not, and I picked the wrong route.

There are days, weeks, months, even years where life in transition will make us feel like we are going backward and getting bucked off a horse. Defeat can feel like the banner of those moments. We may be in shock from the circumstances that have unfolded and led to this transition, and our emotions can be suppressed.

And this is when we have two options: give up *or* learn the lesson and "get back on the horse."

We have the same two options as we arrive at this point in the book.

We can be unsure, scared, or fearful—ready to quit.

Or, we can say we're not ready to give up on this process with God. And trust that there's something in you that still wants to fight for victory as you enter into your next season of life.

And as long as we have that willingness to fight, we have something to work with.

Right here, based on the two choices above, write down where you find yourself today with the transition you are in:

What I love about this spot in Moses's story is that even though he was full of excuses and fear, eventually he resolved in his soul to accept where God was taking him.

But you know what we *don't* see between God and Moses? We don't see Moses verbalize his agreement. There's no, "Yes, God. I will do whatever you say." Instead, we see Moses teaching us that most of the time actions speak louder than words.

And that, my friend, is a lesson we need to learn in the midst of transition. There's a time to be angry, sad, lonely, fearful, wrestling with God, but then . . . there's a time we just need to see what is in our hands today and do the thing we fear the most.

It took me a few weeks to physically recover from getting bucked off Finn. And it took some time to be able to trust him again. But just the other day, I got back on him, and it felt amazing to conquer that fear. Isn't it crazy how conquering one fear can lead to conquering the next?

And now, it's time to conquer yours.

The Liminal Phase of Transition

One of the greatest ways you can fight against the fear that is making you full of excuses is to be able to see the potential in your process today.

> Learning to cultivate what you have in your
> hands and just getting to work can lead to some
> of the greatest breakthroughs in transition.

There's actually a term for this. It's called *liminality*. Here's the definition from dictionary.com: "the transitional period or phase of a rite of passage, during which the participant lacks social status or rank, remains anonymous, shows obedience and humility, and follows prescribed forms of conduct, dress, etc."

The liminal space in transition is one of the hardest to embrace because it requires us to overcome our fears and anxiety and learn to face uncertainty with resilience. The liminal phase can feel uncomfortable, confusing, or downright terrifying. But when you learn to embrace the uncertainty of change and respect the process, you allow yourself to transform into a greater version of yourself and unleash your full potential.

A state of liminality is one where the order of things seems suspended. It's a space between now and the future—the place where transition and transformation occur. Moses cultivated this calling God was giving him during his transition by learning to live well in the liminal space in his life. As he was moving from one season to the next, he had fear, doubt, and discouragement. He made excuses and didn't want to execute the plan. But at the end of the day, Moses did what he needed to do. He let the transition in his life transform him.

> Change can be the soil where our
> confidence in God's leadership grows.

Moses is on the cusp of gaining confidence, and we rarely see any more doubt or questioning of God going forward in his story. We see a man who has learned what he needed to learn and grew how he needed to grow so that the assignment was ready to be conquered.

The liminal phase served him well, and it can for you too.

Pharaoh, Pharaoh, Oh Baby, Let My People Go

I just found out that the origin of the hit '90s youth group song *Pharaoh, Pharaoh* started off as a joke for a senior high school project. But joke's on me, because I am forty-one, and that song still lives rent-free in my head.

And I definitely have been singing it as we head into this next part of Moses's story. (If you don't know what I'm talking about, please search for the song *Pharaoh, Pharaoh* on YouTube and give yourself a little dance break from reading and listen to that song. Bonus points if you learn the motions that go with it.)

As we open our Bibles back up to Exodus 5, a lot of progress has happened with Moses. He has transformed into a leader and is ready to confront Pharaoh.

When you were growing up, did you ever try to confront your parents by asking them why you had to do something? And did they also say those famous words, "BECAUSE I SAID SO"?

My mom said this *all the time*. And ahem, I say it all the time too.

Well, sometimes when we are trying to explain why we are doing what God asked, the only reasoning we can give is, "Because God said so." Often in the Old Testament, we see this mention of the sovereignty of God, but we also see some rationale to help people obey God's commands. But there was no rationalizing with Pharaoh.

Moses says to Pharaoh, "You gotta let my people go because God said so."

But did Moses really expect Pharaoh to say, "Sure, bro, I will let your people go!"? Because Pharaoh doesn't, and it's clear Moses is about to head into a bigger battle than he ever imagined.

But here's something I had a hard time understanding. Exodus 7:3–4 says, "But I will harden Pharaoh's heart, and though

I multiply my signs and wonders in the land of Egypt, Pharaoh will not listen to you."

This feels a little theologically messy. Why would God be the one to harden Pharaoh's heart?

Proverbs 21:1 gives us some insight: "The king's heart is a stream of water in the hand of the Lord; he turns it wherever he will." God is the only one who can change hearts, in either direction. But why here? And why now?

My theology friend David had some thoughts on this. Here's what he said: "The hardening of Pharaoh's heart by God is the mystery of how God's sovereignty interacts with human choice and stubbornness. We see the interaction between the sovereignty of God and the stubborn will of men, but cannot fully comprehend how they interact."

Part of cultivation with God is being willing to seek out answers as to why we don't understand things. But there also has to be a "Because God did it or said it" resolve. When you think about your own season of transition, and specifically those things that seem unfair or wrong, it's easy to wonder why God didn't change the story or someone's heart.

We can't change the past. But we can charge into the future, cultivating those three things we talked about in the last chapter: Truth, Spirit, and faith.

We won't understand it all. Moses certainly didn't either. But that doesn't have to keep us standing still. It may not make sense to us why God would harden Pharaoh's heart multiple times throughout this story, but we have to trust God knew what He was doing.

I also find it comforting to know that God can change hearts. It's what He's doing in our lives through this process. I don't think He's hardening our hearts like Pharaoh's, but He's softening them to be able to receive all that He has for us in our next season of life.

I feel like this can all be summed up in these verses from Proverbs:

> Trust in the LORD with all your heart,
> and do not lean on your own understanding.
> In all your ways acknowledge him,
> and he will make straight your paths.
> Be not wise in your own eyes;
> fear the LORD, and turn away from evil.
> It will be healing to your flesh
> and refreshment to your bones.
>
> Proverbs 3:5–8

Moses is trusting the process, but it's about to get really messy. Up next, one of the most famous stories in Exodus begins to unfold, the ten plagues.

Ten Plagues Because God Ain't Playin'

A few summers ago on the Fixer Upper Farm, I thought we were living through our own version of plagues. We didn't have water turn to blood, but we had flooding, an obnoxious amount of bullfrogs singing to us at night, a pig that just fell over dead with no explanation, flies upon flies upon flies in our barn, and one of our horses gave one of our daughters *lice*.

Y'all, I *cannot* with the lice (cue a gagging sound).

Just those few things were enough to get my attention and cause me angst. I cannot imagine having to live through these ten plagues described in Exodus 7–11.

After Moses gives Pharaoh a fair warning about what's coming if he doesn't let the Hebrews go, here's what the people of Egypt were left to deal with. The plagues are set up in three different sets, all very intentional by God to display something different about Himself. I've given you the verses so you can read and fully understand each plague. I'm also giving you the verses for each of the three purposes for the plagues based on Scripture.

Set One Purpose: for Pharaoh to know that God is the Lord

> Thus says the Lord, "By this you shall know that I am the Lord: behold, with the staff that is in my hand I will strike the water that is in the Nile, and it shall turn into blood."
>
> Exodus 7:17

Plague One: Nile water to turn to blood (Exodus 7:17–18)
Plague Two: frogs (Exodus 8:1–4)
Plague Three: lice or gnats (Exodus 8:16–17)

Set Two Purpose: for Pharaoh to know that God is overseeing and guiding the world

> "But on that day I will set apart the land of Goshen, where my people dwell, so that no swarms of flies shall be there, that you may know that I am the Lord in the midst of the earth."
>
> Exodus 8:22

Plague Four: flies (Exodus 8:20–22)
Plague Five: death of livestock (Exodus 9:1–4)
Plague Six: boils (Exodus 9:8–9)

Set Three Purpose: that Pharaoh would know the extent of God's unmatched power

> "For this time I will send all my plagues on you yourself, and on your servants and your people, so that you may know that there is none like me in all the earth."
>
> Exodus 9:14

Plague Seven: hail (Exodus 9:22-23)
Plague Eight: locusts (Exodus 10:4-5)
Plague Nine: darkness (Exodus 10:21-22)
Plague Ten: death of firstborn (Exodus 11:4-7)

This God who displayed these signs to Pharaoh is the same God we serve today. He hasn't changed. And as we wrap up this transition season of cultivation, we may need to take some time and cultivate our sense of awe and wonder of God.

We don't want a heart like Pharaoh's. One that is stubborn and won't see God for who He is. I know a lot of this section sounds a little scary. Like, why would God do all of those things?

Unfortunately, it's because of evil. And the same evil that we see in the days of Moses is the same evil we see today. And if God was just going to get rid of evil, here's the bad news, He'd also have to get rid of us.

While we don't want a heart like Pharaoh's, I hate to be the one to say this, but we have tendencies just like Pharaoh that are . . . evil.

While the Hebrews experienced many of the effects of the plagues, God provided a way for them to not experience the death of their firstborn. The protection came by placing the blood of a lamb on their doors, as a symbol of God's justice and grace for His chosen people. And from this point on, we will continue to see animal sacrifice, the shedding of blood, between the Israelites and God.

This is where we see the beginning of the annual Israelite holiday called Passover, when the Lord passed over the houses with the blood of the lamb on their doors, allowing their firstborn to live. Everything about this first Passover is described in great detail in Exodus 12. I give you permission to stop reading this book and read that chapter, because it will help you see how important Passover was to God.

God is so neat, because while I'm writing these words my daughter Taylor is actually in Israel right now, and it's almost Passover. I just texted her and asked what it's like there, and she said Jewish people take it very seriously. Like even the grocery stores do not sell any leavened (yeast) bread right now. She also said that many Jewish people have a second set of dishes for the Passover meal, because if even a crumb of bread with yeast is left on it, it's considered unclean.

When Jesus died on the cross, the greatest transition for a soul became available, from death to life. All of the sacrifices were paid on the cross, and following God was not about following traditions. Because, spoiler alert, Moses doesn't save anyone from their evil ways.

We have so much to see in the last section of this book and in our study of Moses. But mainly this—humanity is messy, but Jesus is still the miracle.

Cultivating Until We See It

As we close out this section of the book, I know you may still wonder if you're doing this cultivation season of transition right. I think we all are just like Moses, looking for some sign or wonder to help confirm we're heading in the right direction.

We have seen how to identify our *holy nows*. We saw how intentional God was with Moses and how intentional He is in your life today. We looked out for the fears that could be holding us back from experiencing something new. We are aware of the importance of sometimes doing the things we don't want to do.

And while we may be in this liminal phase of transition, we are letting this process grow us.

You've cultivated a lot in these three chapters.

Don't you wish transition could be mastered in three chapters?

I'm feeling a little disappointed as I write these final words for this section. I got my hopes up this week about this big transition of adoption. There's been a lot of cultivating the last few months, and I thought we were about to be so close to the breakthrough. But, we're not.

We're still in this weird limbo-type place. And I have felt like we have gotten bucked off a horse multiple times. But it's not time to give in, it's time to press in. Even harder.

And so, I continue to get up early and pray prayers of belief over this process. I continue to remind my brain that God can change and move hearts. He sees the injustice in this situation, and He has not turned His head away.

Sometimes we keep asking God to make sense of the things that never do, and God is saying, "Just trust Me, *now*." God is not a "never" God. The only never God gives us is this one:

> Be strong and courageous. Do not be afraid or terrified because of them, for the LORD your God goes with you; he will *never* leave you nor forsake you.
>
> Deuteronomy 31:6 (NIV, emphasis mine)

A transition season of cultivation can be both thrilling and hard. There are good things God is teaching us in this space of our lives. May we continue to cultivate each lesson and live in that liminal space until God says, "*Alright, into the Promised Land we go.*"

In-Between-Seasons
Mini Bible Study

Read Exodus 6 and 7

Who is Aaron?

    A. Moses's uncle

    B. Moses's cousin

    C. Moses's brother

How old does Exodus 7:7 say Moses and Aaron were when they spoke to Pharaoh?

How many plagues were there?

    A. 15

    B. 10

    C. 5

    D. 20

The part about God hardening Pharaoh's heart is one of the most complicated theological parts of our study of Moses. The reality is that the human mind may not be able to fully comprehend this. But here are some verses that might help.

Write out Psalm 10:4

_____

_____

_____

Was Pharaoh prideful? Yes or No

Read Mark 8:17–18

What was the question Jesus asked about their hearts?

_____

_____

_____

Write out Romans 9:17-18

_____

_____

_____

The Bible tells us that Pharaoh also was responsible for hardening his heart (Exodus 7:13). What are some ways our hearts can become hardened?

Read Exodus 12:1–28

Do an internet search and find out, what is unleavened bread?

_____

_____

What was the type of meat to be used?

    A. Beef

    B. Chicken

    C. Lamb

Where were they to place the blood of the lamb (v. 7)?

_____

_____

According to 1 Corinthians 5:7, why do we no longer have to celebrate Passover?

_____

_____

Read Exodus 15—this is the song of Moses.

FINISHED

10

Finished Seasons

One of the hardest parts about owning a farm with animals isn't the coming of them but the going of them. A few years ago, Kris and I decided we were going to become Highland cow breeders. This was a big step for us as first-generation farmers. So we invested some money and purchased our first cows, Autumn and Paisley.

Before I continue with this story, let's have a little farm lesson.

Did you know that you can only call a female cow a *cow*? I had no idea, and the real farmers of America definitely let me know I was saying the wrong thing as I would describe all of our cattle as cows.

Cows that have never been bred are called heifers, and if you get a male, it's called a bull.

But a bull can become what's called a steer by getting the little snip-snip procedure (castration). Bull calves must be made into steers in order to stay on the farm. Otherwise you have inbreeding, and keeping the Highlands' genetics good is important to Kris and me.

So when Autumn had her first baby and it was a bull, I'm not going to lie, I was a little disappointed. Not because he wasn't the cutest thing my eyes have ever seen—oh, he was! But because I knew we were going to have to sell him. We didn't want any steers, because for us, steers just become pets. And Kris Koziarz has told me enough times, we have too many pets out here!

Which is why about six months after he was born, I found myself sitting in an arena during a Highland auction, watching two bidders go neck and neck over our fluffy little dun-colored guy, George. They saw his bloodline and his calm temperament because we'd worked so much with him, and they knew he was a good buy.

And then, the auctioneer hit his gavel and said, "Sold!" and pointed to a woman sitting near the front on the bleachers. The arena clapped, and then... the tears began to well up in my eyes.

I knew our season with George was officially done.

The excitement of finding out Autumn was pregnant, watching him be born, thinking at first *he* was a *she* and naming him Georgia. Only to rename him a few days later, after we discovered we were showing our first-generation farmer roots by getting that gender wrong!

I started thinking back to when we halter trained him. Oh, what an experience that was of teaching him to wear a halter and be led by a lead rope. His midnight escapes from the barnyard ... oh mercy. Autumn's loud mooing would alert us he was out and would wake us up from our sleep. Often we'd find ourselves chasing him down in the pouring rain. Weaning him from Autumn. Learning how to tag his ear and give him his first shots. His snuggles and the way he became part of our little herd.

Our job was finished. And as we handed him over to his new owners, I was proud of us. We did it. We sold our first registered Highland.

But even now as I'm typing this out, I feel a little leak coming from my eyes.

Finished seasons have the opportunity to leave us full of gratitude, being proud of what was accomplished and looking back in satisfaction. But it doesn't mean we won't have some strong emotions and still look ahead wondering what's next.

Looking backward is good when it becomes the thing that propels us forward.

As we head into the final section of this book, we'll be working through the final transition season: finished. I would tend to believe everyone can identify with this season, because we've all finished something.

Whether it was our own graduation, having a baby and watching them grow up, completing a project, or doing all we could in a relationship that had to end . . . everyone can think of a time when we knew: *I'm finished with this.*

But there can also be a tension of not knowing when a season is finished. Some of us are there now, and this is our current struggle with transition, knowing if something is finished in our lives.

This fourth section is the last season we'll work through in this book: a transition season of finished.

Moses has a lot to teach us about what it means to finish seasons well. Before we get into those lessons, let's spend just a little more time understanding what a finished season is.

The Question of Finished

When I released the book *5 Habits of a Woman Who Doesn't Quit*, the number-one question I repeatedly received was, "How do I know when I am supposed to quit something?" It's a valid question. This question is also an important part of the many seasons our lives offer us: how do we know when a season is done?

There is a difference between quitting a season and finishing a season well. Quitting means we throw in the towel and walk away. Finishing means just that, it's finished.

Finishing seasons doesn't mean it ends perfectly, but it can end peacefully.

You've probably heard the advice to begin a project with the end in mind. I understand this sentiment, but sometimes it's hard to see the end at the beginning or even in the middle.

I've found that living our lives in faith means that sometimes God calls us into places that don't reveal the ending in the beginning.

A few years ago, I interviewed a woman who had served for over twenty years in a well-known women's ministry. She was beginning the transition out of this position, and I was curious to know how she was handling things. We talked for over an hour, and I could sense the tension in her soul with this transition.

On one hand, there was comfort knowing the woman who was replacing her was incredible. She was full of fresh ideas, was so eager to learn, and wanted to carry forward the legacy of this ministry.

But she was sad too. Twenty years of relationships, dreams, visions, conferences, and building a phenomenal leadership team was hard to release. Thankfully, she knew it was time to leave. I asked her how she knew, and she said, "God has confirmed it again and again."

She had seen leaders hold on to things too long, and their teams and families suffered because of it. There can be a scarcity mindset when someone's season ends. It's a type of thinking that convinces us there's nothing better than what we had. And if that mindset isn't dealt with, it can cause hard-to-repair problems. Things like severed relationships, people leaving an organization because of unhealthy leadership, or even a drastic decline in effectiveness.

This wise leader wanted to finish well, and even though—in the beginning—she had no end in mind, the signs of her season ending were clear. She taught me there will be confirmation when it's the right time to finish a season in our lives.

When someone quits before God has fulfilled His plans for that season, you don't find a lot of confirmation for the quitter. Usually it's the opposite; people try to convince the person *not to quit.*

But when our season is coming to a healthy finish, often other people can see it too. Let's talk about some of the signs or clues that might indicate it's time to start thinking about finishing well.

Possible Signs of Being Finished

Based on some research I've done and conversations I've had with people who have finished seasons well, below are a few signs that could reveal your season is coming to a close:

- What used to make you feel free now makes you feel frustrated
- You find yourself doing as little as possible
- There's constant conflict around this situation
- You get easily irritated with things you used to love
- What worked well in one season of life no longer works well

- You may feel restless and unsettled, wondering if there's something else for you
- God may be placing a new desire, dream, or even a burden to carry in your heart
- You are out of ideas and options to keep things moving forward

These are just some of the signs that we are entering a finished transition season. But unlike the other transition seasons we've studied, sometimes this one is not as clear. For sure some markers are obvious, like graduations, sending kids off to school or their moving out of the house, jobs or projects being completed, or relationships that end.

But the beginnings of some finished seasons are often hazy, and we may not even recognize it. I recently walked alongside a young friend of mine as she experienced a really messy breakup. Her heart was shattered after her long relationship ended. After talking it through, she said looking back, there were many red flags or signs.

She had ignored all the signs because she didn't think she could do better than him.

My heart connected with hers, because breakup or no breakup, sometimes we hold on to seasons thinking it's our best or only option. Other times we're afraid to admit it's time for that chapter to close. And sometimes we doubt God has anything new or better planned for us.

Moses has quite a bit to teach us about this and what it means to finish seasons well. So let's jump back into our study of his life.

Fight the Right Enemy

As we open back up to Exodus 13, the plagues are over, and finally Pharaoh agrees to let the Israelites go. They begin their journey to the Promised Land (Canaan), and it seems like they can all exhale . . . but only for a moment.

Because just a little while after the Israelites leave, Pharaoh's heart hardens again (Exodus 14:4–8) and he loads up his chariots and his soldiers to go after the Israelites.

They all arrive at the climax of this story, the Red Sea.

As Pharaoh's army approaches, the Hebrews are full of fear. They are angry at Moses and believe he led them into a death trap (Exodus 14:11–12). As Pharaoh and his army approach, Moses is placed in a divine leadership position with the Israelites. He has to lead them through their fears with his faith.

And this is where we see one of my favorite verses in this story:

> And Moses said to the people, "Fear not, stand firm, and see the salvation of the LORD, which he will work for you today. For the Egyptians whom you see today, you shall never see again. The LORD will fight for you, and you have only to be silent."
>
> Exodus 14:13–14

We are seeing a very mature and wise version of Moses. This man who God developed as a child, separated as a man, and cultivated into a calling only he could do. He's not quite there yet, but Moses is about to enter his finished season.

Moses doesn't know it, but this is one of many hurdles he'll have to face before finishing this season well. So, at this pivotal moment, Moses tells his people to do three things:

1. Do not be afraid.
2. Stand firm.
3. Be still.

There is tension in this transition space where the Israelites find themselves. And these three instructions are a powerful lesson for them, as they are all entering into a finished season. Getting there required some action. And sometimes actions can make us feel like we are somehow in control of the situation. So being still often feels conflicting in a finished season.

Often in finished seasons of transition, people (including ourselves) may do or say things that feel hurtful when they get confused as to who their "enemy" really is.

I served under a leader in a church setting who didn't want an individual on their team anymore because they seemed stuck in the past. The teammate wanted to keep doing things the way they had always been done, while the leader was trying to move the team forward. This created tension.

Instead of having an honest conversation with this one person about their season being finished, the leader decided to make up a whole set of impossible rules for the entire team to follow. The hope was the person they wanted to step down would.

This actually backfired, and the leader lost several valuable teammates—and the person they wanted to step down didn't. The leader panicked, and in their own fear said some hurtful things to this person, which only made the situation worse.

This was years ago, and I can tell you, there's still tension on that team. When we don't face finished seasons head-on with grace and love, they can end disastrously or drag on for years, making everyone around us miserable.

One of the things that stood out to me as I was studying the Israelites' reaction to Moses is they were trying to make Moses the enemy. They said things to him like, "You should've let us die in Egypt!" (Exodus 14:12). Moses could have said harsh things back, but he knew who the real enemy was: Pharaoh.

Transition seasons (especially finished ones) can cause us to fear and say and do things we normally wouldn't. We can start to think of people as the enemy.

When my mom was dying, I had a hard time accepting it and often looked at the doctor who was over my mom's care as my enemy. Sometimes I would say things to my husband like, "If he would have caught this or done this . . ." Her season on earth was done, but I didn't want to let her go.

> **Sometimes the enemy is a "pharaoh," sometimes it's Satan, and sometimes . . . it's us.**

When we can't see where God is taking us and we feel stuck in this seemingly never-ending now, we will have to fight. We have to fight to let go of what needs to go, fight for the good plans God has for us ahead, and fight not to see the wrong enemy.

But remember, as Moses said to the Israelites, sometimes the fight looks like this:

> The LORD will fight for you, and *you have only to be silent.*
>
> Exodus 14:14 (emphasis mine)

The God Who Split Seas

Moses has done some growing up. He's still in process for sure, but we see the wise and confident version of Moses represented in this part of the story.

He knows the plan, and he knows God will come through.

And then we see the full circle of Moses's transition seasons of development, separation, and cultivation come into play.

Remember what we learned in the last section of the book about looking to see what we have in our hands today? That it could be a clue as to where God is taking us next? Look what God reminds Moses he has:

> The LORD said to Moses, "Why do you cry to me? Tell the people of Israel to go forward. *Lift up your staff*, and stretch out your hand over the sea and divide it, that the people of Israel may go through the sea on dry ground. And I will harden the hearts of the Egyptians so that they shall go in after them, and I will get glory over Pharaoh and all his host, his chariots, and his horsemen."
>
> Exodus 14:15–17 (emphasis mine)

The staff. It's still there. And it's still what God is using.

When you feel like you are entering into a finished transition season, it might be tempting to think that if this season ends, all of the good ends too. The gifts, the talents, the hard work you've put in, it may feel like it's all going to disappear.

But may we, like Moses with his staff, see that in every season of life God calls us into, He will keep using what we've got.

> Becoming surrendered to a season
> that is finished doesn't mean we stop
> being available to be used by God.

Moses takes what he has, that staff, then stretches out his hand, and God comes through for Moses and the Israelites like He has this entire story. The waters of the sea begin to part, and so begins the long crossing of the Red Sea. I was surprised to learn from my theology friend David that this crossing would have taken half the night. It was over ten miles across. Think of the women, children, animals, carts toting all their belongings, and what it would have taken to get across as quickly as possible.

The Israelites finish the crossing, the waters close in on Pharaoh's army, and finally, the Israelites are safe.

Thus the Lᴏʀᴅ saved Israel that day from the hand of the Egyptians, and Israel saw the Egyptians dead on the seashore. Israel
saw the great power that the Lᴏʀᴅ used against the Egyptians,
so the people feared the Lᴏʀᴅ, and they believed in the Lᴏʀᴅ and
in his servant Moses.

Exodus 14:30–31

Again and again, we see this theme throughout this story.
Moses is a hero, but not THE hero. One of the most fascinating
things about studying the Bible is how we can clearly see it point
to Jesus through every story.

We can see the foreshadowing of Jesus here at the Red Sea
parting, because there would come a point when it would seem
as though all was lost. And as Jesus died on the cross, it seemed
like it was over.

But God stretched out His arms over humanity. And three
days later, Jesus would rise from the dead and then later as-
cend into heaven. Because of the act of mercy on the cross,
the enemy has already been defeated. And now, Jesus sits at the
right hand of the Father, interceding for us. It's a reflection of
the way we cross from here to there, with God.

God is the same God today as He was to Moses. And in the
midst of your own seasons of transitions, it may feel as though
an enemy is chasing you to your own Red Sea. And while he is,
you are not facing him alone (1 Peter 5:8).

One might think that after crossing the Red Sea for freedom,
life would be a lot easier for the Israelites. It seems like the season is finished, and in one way, it is. But in many ways, it's not.
They would spend the next forty years wandering through the
wilderness. Being mad at God, mad at Moses, and mad at their
circumstances.

Remember the goal was to take the people from Egypt to the
Promised Land, in Canaan. And while God provided the plan,

He never gave an exact timeline. The Israelites would continue to be challenging people for Moses to lead, and their process would determine the timeline of their journey.

Despite the Israelites complaining and grumbling, God was kind. There were two things given to the Israelites during this journey:

1. God's daily provision. The Lord would send manna, which is bread from heaven, each day (Exodus 16:4). In our mini Bible study at the end of this section, we'll spend some more time unpacking this. God would also provide water from a rock (Exodus 17).
2. God's presence. While they were traveling, there was a cloud by day and a fire by night that held the presence of God.

And the Lord went before them by day in a pillar of cloud to lead them along the way, and by night in a pillar of fire to give them light, that they might travel by day and by night. The pillar of cloud by day and the pillar of fire by night did not depart from before the people.

Exodus 13:21-22

Sometimes in any season of transition, including finished seasons, we go with someone else. And sometimes we have to go alone. But God is already there, in every circumstance.

Psalm 23 is one of the most famous psalms in Scripture. It paints a powerful picture of how God's provision and His presence are with us in the midst of transition:

The Lord is my shepherd; I shall not want.
He makes me lie down in green pastures.
He leads me beside still waters.

He restores my soul.
He leads me in paths of righteousness
for his name's sake.
Even though I walk through the valley of the shadow of
      death,
I will fear no evil,
for you are with me;
your rod and your staff,
they comfort me.

Psalm 23:1–4

When we feel alone, the Shepherd is always there.

When it feels hard to discern the future, He leads us.

When it feels like we can't make a decision, even if our life depended on it, He guides us.

When we feel hesitation to take the next step, He walks with us.

When we feel fearful, His rod and staff protect us.

People are always looking for fresh, new, and exciting concepts to solve the problems they are facing. Maybe it's my age or my life season or just the chaos in this world right now, but when I'm feeling like my season is finished with something, I don't need a five-step formula to find my way. I need this never-changing, always present, same God. I need God to meet me in the midst of my now.

We don't need a new revelation of God, we need to remember the God of yesterday is the same God today.

As we close out this chapter, I wanted to give you some space to process and pray through your own transition season of being finished. Because we've established that seasons will keep changing, I think this is a healthy practice to do again and again.

So find ten minutes of time, grab a journal, and process with God the following:

A Guided, Journaled Prayer Time for Finished Seasons

1. Begin by writing down everything you are grateful for about this season.
2. Write out all the good things this season brought you and others.
3. What are the things you've said in fear, maybe to yourself or others? Write those down.
4. Is there anyone you need to apologize to? Is there anything you need to confess to God? Spend some time letting God show you what needs to be changed in your heart.
5. What is at least one lesson this season has taught you? Write it out in as much detail as you can, and ask God for help to gain even more wisdom from this season.
6. Write out any verses that have helped you through this season.
7. Close by journaling what you would like your next season to look like. Ask God if it aligns with His heart. And ask Him for grace as you prepare for the next season of your life.

11

Finish Lines and Full Circles

A few years ago, my husband and I started marriage counseling. Nothing was drastically wrong, but you know after twenty-ish years of looking at the same person each day you can start to find yourself annoyed with their habits, like the way they slurp their cereal milk. Or you just find yourself slowly growing apart. We both recognized the need to have someone speak wisdom into our lives.

One of the things the counselor said to us was, "Wow. I have never counseled two more opposite people; you guys literally have nothing in common." Gee, thanks for pointing out the obvious.

So he challenged both of us to find ways to come into each other's world. Kris agreed to try to learn more about horses since that is an interest of mine, and I agreed to give running a try since that is something Kris really loves to do.

But you know, I don't do things small. Like maybe it would have been wise to say, "Let's start with a 5K."

No ma'am, I signed up for a HALF MARATHON (13.1 miles). Which was the hardest physical and mental thing I had ever trained for. I thought I was prepared for it, but on the day of the race when I reached mile ten, I began to question the entire existence of my life.

I felt like I was going to die.

My entire body was shaking, it was really hot, and I didn't think I could finish. I stopped and drank a ton of water, too much water. But it seemed to give me the strength to keep going, and so I continued on.

Until I realized I needed to go to the bathroom from drinking so much water.

The problem was that I knew there was a time limit to finish the race before they kicked me off the course. I didn't think I had time to stop. And so I made the decision to just deal with the uncomfortable feeling and get to the finish line.

But then, I sneezed.

And those of you who can understand what happens to a woman's bladder for the rest of her life after she pushes a baby out of her body fully grasp why this was problematic. A full bladder + exhausted body + a sneeze = disaster.

I will spare you the details of all that transpired in the next thirty seconds, but I knew I had a choice. Either I quit or I did whatever I had to do, including running in soaked pants and a humiliated face.

Some people say that crossing the finish line after a long race is a magical moment. But, y'all, for me, it wasn't. All I could think of was *I am just so glad that's over!* I was proud of my ability to persevere and do something that was part of Kris's world, but I only felt like celebrating for a minute. I was more concerned with how quickly I could get to a shower!

Sometimes finishing a season well looks like a big celebration. I think about a post I recently saw of a woman who retired after thirty years of teaching. There were balloons, confetti, a big party, and fabulous speeches.

And then other times, finishing well is just getting across the finish line with a little "woo" and no desire to ever do that again.

So no matter how you are feeling about your own finish line, the fact that you are finishing a season of your life to the best of your ability is something to cheer for. But it is also OK if you are just barely getting across that line and would never want to do it again.

The Israelites are crossing their own finish line: one season is finished, but they are about to be in that transition space for a long time—forty years to be exact.

Purpose, Plans, and Commands

The Israelites were both celebrating and soaking in their new reality after they crossed over the Red Sea. We see in Exodus 15 their song of celebration with Moses, but then, in the very next chapter, they are right back to the reality of their new now: the wilderness. And this transition space is filled with grumbling, complaining, and fear.

Moses is doing his best to lead the Israelites into the Promised Land, but it is challenging. As they cross the end of the Red Sea, they make their way to Mt. Sinai. The same sacred place Moses met God at the burning bush for this assignment.

What a full-circle moment for Moses. He was doing it. Leading his people and obeying God with each step.

The presence of God that was with them this entire journey by the cloud and fire now ascended to the top of Mt. Sinai. Moses went up to meet with God and get some instructions for order and purpose for the Israelites, because things were complicated.

And oh my, God has a lot of instructions to give Moses for the people.

First, God calls them to a really high place. To become a "kingdom of priests."

> "Now therefore, if you will indeed obey my voice and keep my covenant, you shall be my treasured possession among all peoples, for all the earth is mine; and you shall be to me a kingdom of priests and a holy nation." These are the words that you shall speak to the people of Israel.
>
> Exodus 19:5–6

What does that mean exactly? Well, it was basically an assignment to be a mediator of the knowledge of God to the rest of the world. This was their purpose, even though their location, jobs, and lifestyle would continue to change. It was to be the core of who they were.

And no matter what season of life or transition seasons we are in, you and I have this same assignment today, to be a mediator between the Truth we have come to believe and the rest of the world.

> But you are a chosen race, a royal priesthood, a holy nation, a people for his own possession, that you may proclaim the excellencies of him who called you out of darkness into his marvelous light.
>
> 1 Peter 2:9

So when we're not sure what to do next, this is always our *now*. To be the people God has set apart in this generation to represent Him and His Truth well. We do this by letting God develop us, separate us from what needs to go, and cultivate His Word and presence in our lives. That's the ultimate finish line we should always be pursuing.

And when we find ourselves like the Israelites, grumbling and complaining in our *now*, we need to ask God to bring us back to this core place. Because here in that kind of *now*, there is always direction, wisdom, and peace to be found.

His grace calls us into this high place in our lives in every season. But God is both law and grace.

And the Israelites were in need of some law and order.

In the Old Testament, we see three different types of law represented: moral, civil, and ceremonial. Most of the ceremonial laws do not relate to us today because our salvation through Jesus no longer binds us to them.

The civil and moral laws, however, are still a good guide for us when it comes to our conduct and how we live our lives. So we can learn much from studying the 613 laws we see represented in the Bible.

We don't have the capacity here to study this in depth, but if you want to take this deeper, I highly recommend studying Exodus, Leviticus, Numbers, and Deuteronomy through a trusted source like the First 5 app through Proverbs 31 Ministries.

But there's no way we could skip over one of the things Moses is most known for, the Ten Commandments. These commands from God are still valuable for us today, especially when we are in the midst of transition, because they help us stay grounded in God's character.

The Ten Commandments

The Ten Commandments would fall into the category of moral law, and the two places we see them written in the Bible are Exodus 20:2–17 and Deuteronomy 5:6–21. Here are the Ten

Commandments, and I highly recommend you take some time to read the verses that go with each of them.

1. Have no other gods before God (Exodus 20:3).
2. Do not make for yourself an idol in the form of anything in heaven above or on the earth beneath or in the waters below (Exodus 20:4).
3. Don't misuse God's name (Exodus 20:7).
4. Remember the Sabbath day and keep it holy (Exodus 20:8).
5. Honor your mother and father (Exodus 20:12).
6. Do not murder (Exodus 20:13).
7. Don't commit adultery (Exodus 20:14).
8. Don't steal (Exodus 20:15).
9. Don't give false testimony against your neighbor (Exodus 20:16).
10. Don't covet (Exodus 20:17).

Proof that the Ten Commandments still apply to us is that Jesus references them in Luke 18:20: "You know the commandments: 'Do not commit adultery, Do not murder, Do not steal, Do not bear false witness, Honor your father and mother.'"

There are other places we see the Ten Commandments represented in the New Testament. The chart below shows you some verses to look up to see the connection:

Command	New Testament References
You shall have no other gods before me	Matthew 4:10; Luke 4:8; Revelation 14:7
You shall not make for yourself an idol	John 4:23; Acts 15:20; 1 Corinthians 6:9–10; Galatians 5:19–20; Ephesians 5:5; Colossians 3:5

Command	New Testament References
You shall not misuse the name of the Lord your God	Matthew 5:33–37; 1 Timothy 6:1; James 2:7; 5:12
Remember the Sabbath day and keep it holy	Luke 4:16; 23:55–56; Acts 17:1–2; 18:4; Hebrews 4:9
Honor your father and mother	Matthew 15:4–9; 19:19; Mark 10:19; Luke 18:20; Romans 1:29–30; Ephesians 6:1–3
You shall not murder	Matthew 5:21–22; 19:18; Mark 10:19; Luke 18:20; Romans 1:29–30; 13:9
You shall not commit adultery	Matthew 5:27–28; 19:18; Mark 10:11–12, 19; Luke 16:18; 18:20; Romans 7:2–3; 13:9
You shall not steal	Matthew 19:18; Mark 10:19; Luke 18:20; Romans 13:9; Ephesians 4:28; 1 Peter 4:15; Revelation 9:21
You shall not lie	Matthew 19:18; Mark 10:19; Luke 18:20; Acts 5:3–4; Ephesians 4:25
You shall not covet	Luke 12:15; Romans 1:29; 7:7; 13:9; Ephesians 5:3, 5

One of the things I have tried to instill in each of my daughters—and I will also with my sons too when they come home—is to know the character of God. Just the other day my daughter sent me a text during her lunch break at school. She was upset that in one of her classes they were building a political case about a law in America, and no one was building their case like she was. She said, "Why am I like the only one who believes like I do?"

I tried to help her understand that the way we've raised her is based on biblical values. And the reality of the world we live in is that most people don't build their lives based on biblical Truth.

Part of building a life on biblical Truth means that your values come from the Bible, not from what feels or sounds good based on the culture around us.

These moral commands from God are still valid for today.

In a sense, the world is on its way to the finish line, and when Jesus returns, the race will be over. We all play a role in our generation's finishing well by building a legacy of faith in and around us.

Part of finishing seasons well doesn't mean we live perfect lives and follow God's every command to a T. That's impossible.

But so often we as Christians become known for what we're against. And the Ten Commandments offer us a foundation for things God is for.

God is for:

Worship of Him only

Removing the idols in our lives

Keeping His name holy and set apart

Weekly rest and worship for our lives

Honoring our parents

Life

Commitment in marriage

Not taking people's stuff

Truth

Being content with what He gives us

The reality is, we are no different than the Israelites in our need for God. The human heart has not changed since Eve found herself in the Garden of Eden. Sin entered and sin remains.

As we head to our own finish lines, both in seasons and in our lives here on this earth, we need the grace of God through Jesus and His commands throughout Scripture for us to finish well.

I'm thankful God is a God of both law and grace, because following every law and command in the Bible is impossible. And Jesus came to fulfill both.

We will see in a little bit Moses's need for grace in his life. And we'll see that even before Jesus, God's grace was found all over the Old Testament.

Because He's the same God.

When we don't build our lives on the character of God, it can have consequences in our lives and the generations to follow.

Several have noted, "What one generation
tolerates, the next embraces."

That quote hits me hard when I feel like skipping church, prayer time, or Bible study, or quitting something in my life I know I'm supposed to press through. I have a responsibility, and I'm the only one who can take responsibility for my assignments.

We may not impact the entire world
with the decisions we make each day,
but we impact our entire world.

I think if Moses had any idea of the impact his decisions and leadership would have for thousands of years, it would have totally freaked him out. There was enough pressure on him just to lead the people in front of him well.

As Moses received the Ten Commandments, he also received something else incredible: directions for building the tabernacle—the place that would become the earthly dwelling place of God. Something so special and unforgettable for generations to come.

Tents and Church on the Farm

A few summers ago, we had a church reach out to us about hosting their Sunday church service on our farm for a few weeks while they found somewhere new to meet. Kris and I try to live our lives in a posture of being open to what God is doing, so we did what we always do: we said yes. Then we jumped in full speed ahead to help this church however we could.

Kris found a large outdoor tent for them to meet under while the summer sun was at its hottest. It took an army of people to set up the tent, but once it was up it felt like it had a purpose beyond just giving some shade on Sunday mornings.

Then I had an idea I sensed was straight from God.

A few of my friends and I have done several revivals out here on our farm. We've seen God do the neatest things through these revivals, and I knew once the tent was up this was an excellent opportunity to do another.

So I rallied our team, and we began planning a tent revival.

While the tent was up, almost daily I would find myself being drawn to go and sit and pray in this tent.

At the time I was studying Moses and the tent (sanctuary) that changed everything for him and the Israelites. Having a tent in my front yard definitely helped bring this part of Moses's story to life.

When Adam and Eve sinned in the Garden of Eden, which was the first sanctuary, they lost a lot, including the ability to be safe and secure in God's garden. But the greatest thing that was lost was the presence of God (Genesis 3). Moses's story is one of deliverance but also one of redemption, because this is where the fulfillment of God's promise to bring back His presence to His people came.

> And let them make me a sanctuary, that I may dwell in their midst.
>
> Exodus 25:8

God is a God of order, and when you read about the laws and the tabernacle you can clearly see that. The tabernacle is mentioned three hundred twenty times in the Bible. The first mention of the tabernacle is in Exodus 25:9, the last is Revelation

15:5. Since we are just doing an overview of Moses's life through this book, I encourage you to spend some time reading Exodus 25–27 and 35–40 to learn more about the tabernacle.

But for several hundred years until King Solomon would build the temple, the tabernacle is where the Ten Commandments were kept, in the Ark of the Covenant. I love what Exodus 33:7–9 says about the tent (the tabernacle) that went with them each step of their journey:

> Now Moses used to take the tent and pitch it outside the camp, far off from the camp, and he called it the tent of meeting. And everyone who sought the Lord would go out to the tent of meeting, which was outside the camp. Whenever Moses went out to the tent, all the people would rise up, and each would stand at his tent door, and watch Moses until he had gone into the tent. When Moses entered the tent, the pillar of cloud would descend and stand at the entrance of the tent, and the Lord would speak with Moses.
>
> Exodus 33:7–9

The tabernacle is full of symbolism, all that points to Jesus. And because of Jesus, God is not contained to a building or structure.

> And the Word became flesh and dwelt among us, and we have seen his glory, glory as of the only Son from the Father, full of grace and truth.
>
> John 1:14

Still, there is something powerful that happens when we gather corporately to worship God. When we are in the midst of life's transitions, worship and seeking God's presence is so important. When I read about the tabernacle and the process Moses went through to speak with the Lord, I can feel the holiness and desperation in his steps of obedience to seek God. It seems like the closer he got to his own finish line, the closer he drew to God.

And sometimes I just feel like we as modern-day followers of Jesus become so complacent about the holiness of God's presence. Like, I have full access to God all day long, but some days it feels like too much to even find ten minutes to sit and pray. Or how a wealth of information about the Bible is at our fingertips through the internet, but some days I'd rather just check out from life and fill my mind with things on the internet that entertain my brain rather than educate it.

While we may not have much control over the way seasons ebb and flow in our lives, we have much control over the way we steward our days. And when we study the time and the process that Moses and the Israelites put into seeking God, we should feel challenged by that.

The night of the revival came, and there was a woman who came with her teenage sons. They were going through a really difficult time, and the boys were struggling. But at one point during worship, the mom turned to the side to try to find one of the boys, and she panicked for a second because she couldn't see him.

But then, as she turned all the way around, she saw him flat on his face in the grass, worshiping Jesus. The young man told his mom later that night it was the first time he had felt the presence of God in a really long time, and he didn't want it to end.

None of us really wanted that night to end, and it's almost been two years since that revival. My friends and I still talk about it a lot, because that's what happens when we want more of God's presence.

Eventually, the church that was meeting here found a permanent place to meet and the tent came down. Church on the farm was finished, and that season came to an end.

Because the tent was up for about five weeks, the grass beneath it died. At first, I was a little frustrated with it because it was an eyesore. But it's been two years since that tent was up and the grass still hasn't come back fully. And I hope it doesn't anytime soon. That dead area of grass is a reminder: *something holy happened here.*

Church on the farm was temporary, just like the tabernacle Moses built would be. But even today, that revival night lingers in the hearts of those who experienced the presence of God, just like the holiness of the tabernacle lingers for us.

12

Go Be Great

There are a lot of sad stories in the Bible, but where we're going next in our study of Moses is for sure one of the saddest. After nearly forty years of wandering in the wilderness, they are close to reaching Canaan. They have gone from Egypt to the Red Sea to Mt. Sinai, and now they are to Kadesh, which on a map looks like just a few jumps into Canaan, the Promised Land.

Numbers 20:1 says that Moses's wife Zipporah dies and is buried. There is a grief Moses is dealing with, but he also has more grumbling from the Israelites to deal with. They are mad, again, this time because there is not any water for themselves or their cattle.

Having to fill up water tanks for our animals daily on the Fixer Upper Farm allows me to have compassion for their fear. The animals did need water to survive.

But where I shake my head a little is when I see them once again blaming Moses for bringing them to this place. They have seen God provide every step of the way. And they still don't trust Him.

Oh, but wait. I just did the same thing yesterday.

There's a worship song called "Goodness of God," and in it are lines about God's faithfulness and goodness. I get tears in my eyes when I sing those lines, because I truly can look back on my entire life and see the hand of God.

Back to yesterday. Kris and I had a huge argument. It was a dumb fight, and at the core, I was blaming him for my own fears, much like the Israelites did to Moses. I said to him, "I just don't understand what God is doing, and I'm mad."

How quickly I forget.

And I imagine there's at least one other person reading this who can relate. We see God come through again and again, but we still don't trust.

I love Moses's response and reaction to the Israelites.

> Then Moses and Aaron went from the presence of the assembly to the entrance of the tent of meeting and fell on their faces. And the glory of the LORD appeared to them . . .
>
> Numbers 20:6

Can you imagine what our lives would look like if that would become the posture of our hearts when things feel out of control and we lack direction? To fall on our faces before God. Wow.

And the Lord has the answer like He always does. But read this closely, because this is where Moses's ending begins.

> Take the staff, and assemble the congregation, you and Aaron your brother, and tell the rock before their eyes to yield its water. So you shall bring water out of the rock for them and give drink to the congregation and their cattle.
>
> Numbers 20:8

This is the second time we see God using the rock to provide water for the people and their animals. But notice, this time, God gives a different command. Instead of Moses using his staff to strike the rock like he did in Exodus 17, he is supposed to *speak* to the rock.

And I don't know what made Moses do what he did next. Maybe he was frustrated. Maybe he had too much grief in his heart. I don't know. But my heart hurts as I read this next part.

> And Moses lifted up his hand and struck the rock with his staff twice, and water came out abundantly, and the congregation drank, and their livestock. And the Lord said to Moses and Aaron, "Because you did not believe in me, to uphold me as holy in the eyes of the people of Israel, therefore you shall not bring this assembly into the land that I have given them."
>
> Numbers 20:11-12

And there it is.

Moses would never enter the Promised Land, because God said, "You did not believe in me." It feels kind of harsh, doesn't it? After all, his entire life had led up to this point. And I can't help but wonder how many nights around the fire Moses would sit with Aaron and they would talk about the future, what it would be like to finally be in Canaan and how they would live out the rest of their lives.

And the story gets sadder. Because not only will Moses not enter into the Promised Land, Aaron won't either. And it's for the same reason as Moses, disobedience.

> And when all the congregation saw that Aaron had perished, all the house of Israel wept for Aaron for thirty days.
>
> Numbers 20:29

When It's Time to Go

When my youngest daughter, Kennedy Grace, was in the third grade, I started traveling more for ministry. It was always a juggle to be a good and present mom and to be prepared for an event. One Friday morning I had a speaking event in New Jersey and had to be at the airport pretty early, but I had enough time to drop Kennedy off at school. This was important to her in that phase of her life, and so I did my best to schedule things around dropping her off in the morning.

But she was mad that I was leaving for the weekend to go and teach. So on the way to school, I tried to explain to her that this assignment from God wasn't just for me, it was for our whole family. I couldn't do what I do without their support.

With tears in her eyes, she hopped out of the minivan and began to close the door. She looked at me with eyes leaking and said, "Well, then go be great." And slammed the door and walked off to class.

I called Kris in tears and told him this story. He thought it was cute she said that, and when we went to hang up, he said, "Go be great."

Sometimes I wonder if I've heard from God correctly about this assignment to teach His Word, and there's always this tension inside me. I worry about our family and farm while I'm away. I struggle with feeling insecure about teaching the Bible.

That drop-off with Kennedy was seven years ago now, and almost every time I get ready to teach at an event Kris texts me one thing: *Go be great.*

Those three words somehow give me the confidence I need to do what God has asked me to do. It doesn't mean the process is perfect or that there isn't still tension between being gone and being home.

Kennedy hadn't read about Moses and Aaron, and I don't

know where she got that phrase from, but we are about to see it said to someone we haven't studied about yet.

It's Over and It's Not

The wild thing about Moses's story is that even though he was not going to lead the Israelites into Canaan, he didn't exit the story and give up. God still had work for him to do.

And isn't that a message for us today?

> Just because we think something is finished,
> there may still be work to be done.

Another leader would need to be raised up to lead the Israelites. And there was someone who had been quietly behind the scenes of this story, getting ready for his step into leadership:

And Joshua overwhelmed Amalek and his people with the sword.

Exodus 17:13

Joshua would become the leader of the Israelites, but not until the death of Moses.

There are many verses and chapters to study from the point when Aaron dies to the death of Moses. Moses's life is one I could study for years and still not fully comprehend everything.

But we are reaching the true end of Moses's story here on earth.

In Deuteronomy 34, Moses goes up from the plains of Moab to Mount Nebo. Here God shows him the land that He promised to Abraham, Isaac, and to Jacob (Deuteronomy 1:7–8). And then, it's over.

So Moses the servant of the Lord died there in the land of Moab, according to the word of the Lord, and he buried him in the valley

in the land of Moab opposite Beth-peor; but no one knows the
place of his burial to this day.

Deuteronomy 34:5-6

Oh man, you guys. I'm struggling with this ending. We have
seen Moses come so far, and he literally dies looking at the
promise. I am so sad for him. But it also makes me stop and
think so much about the things I want to see happen in my life.
It causes me to pause in this space of transition in my life and
pray, *God, do whatever you have to do in my life so I don't miss it.*

But when we pray something like that, may we be ready to
respond when God says, "Go."

Moses's story has many lessons for us, but this one, "Do whatever God says," seems to ring the loudest.

But did Moses finish well?

I would say yes. Even though he didn't make it into the Promised Land, Moses made it through the hardest parts of this journey and led his people well. And I think there is a comfort to be
found in this story for those of us who may be looking back on
a season that ended in a way we have regrets about.

And if you feel as though you don't have true closure for a
season that ended differently than you wanted it to, the next
few pages may help you.

The Letter We May Never Send

When we feel like a season of our life ended abruptly or our
feelings have caught us off guard now that it's finished, we may
need to spend some time bringing closure the best we can.

Often finish lines can be filled with unhealed wounds or hurtful circumstances. You may need to say goodbye to something
or someone without ever having the opportunity to do so.

I've experienced this several times in my life. Once was when

I got married. I was a young nineteen-year-old bride, and our marriage was quick, only six weeks after I found out I was pregnant. Life transitioned fast, and one day I found myself holding a newborn baby girl while everyone else my age was experiencing college and the newfound freedom of being out of their parents' home.

For several years I was resentful of my life, and it came out in the worst ways. And so I began to write letters to my younger self in my journal. I said goodbye to things that hurt me from that season. I expressed gratitude for what I learned, and somehow I became whole again.

That newborn baby girl has grown into a woman now.

And the other day she said to me, "Sometimes I feel bad for you because you never got to experience all the fun adventurous life of being a young adult."

Because I healed from that season, I don't feel like I missed a thing. And watching my girls grow up and do all the things I never got to experience is even better than me doing it.

Another example was when a church we had been a part of for a few years dissolved as we knew it. The pastor and everyone on staff left because of some really complicated and unhealthy circumstances. I felt lost after spending so much time building relationships and serving at this church. It ended so abruptly that it caught me off guard.

As we started to find a new church, I was skeptical of the process, because I had experienced hurt without closure. I kept longing for what we had at that church, but it was no more. In order to move forward, my emotions needed closure as that season was finished.

And so I journaled and wrote the things my soul needed to say but my lips didn't need to speak.

Sometimes it feels like we don't have the ability to bring closure to a season. But I have the best news for you. You actually do have time, and there is a way to bring closure to something in your life that needs it.

Not everyone loves to write. Even sending emails can feel like it's going to steal someone's joy for the day. But because you are reading this, and we are at the end of this book, I know something about you.

You know that words matter.

If you are nodding your head in agreement, please stay open to what I'm going to ask you to do.

And as we close out our journey together, I want to give you the opportunity to bring closure to something in your life if you need to. It's called *writing a letter you may never send*.

Writing a letter you may never send could be one of the most healing things you ever do. And below are some steps to help you do this.

First, find a time when you can be absolutely alone.

No phone, no social media, no one knocking on your door. Mommas of littles, I know this is hard, but maybe ask a friend to help, even if it's just for thirty minutes.

Begin by addressing the letter to the person, place, or thing that has ended in your life. You may even want to address it as a season—for example, To: my season of being a student or To: my season of being a stay-at-home mom.

Recognize and call out exactly what happened. Be specific and write what you experienced, what you felt, and any unmet dreams or expectations about this place of ending in your life.

Ask yourself an honest question about your part in the process of that season ending. Is there anything you wish you would have done differently or not at all? Write like you would dance when no one is watching you. Be free and be vulnerable.

Write out your goodbye to whatever or whoever needs to be said goodbye to. I would also encourage you to include a prayer. Close the season, and finish it well in your soul.

When you are done writing it, put it away for at least one day.

After a day, or however much time you determine you need, go back and read the letter aloud as you would if that person or season or whatever it is were looking you square in the face.

And then you get to decide what to do with that letter.

You can burn it or keep it if you feel like you may need to read it a few more times. You can also send the letter, if that's a possibility and you feel you need to do it.

Fruit, Faithfulness, and Who Follows

The death and end of Moses's life is sad, for sure. But one of the ways we can identify if someone has finished well is by the fruit that is left from their lives. And Moses left a lot of good fruit behind. It's why we're still talking about him today.

But another question I had when I read this was *Why did God bury Moses?* There are some theories out there, and one is that God knew the Israelites were prone to become idol worshipers again.

Had Moses had a tombstone, they could have turned it into a shrine and worshiped it.

There are other theologians who consider the option that maybe God preserved Moses's body, and he will be one of the two witnesses we see mentioned in Revelation 11. But the reality is, no one knows.

But what we do know is that God still had a plan for the Israelites. And it was time for that leader who had been behind the scenes to rise up and lead the way.

> And Joshua the son of Nun was full of the spirit of wisdom, for Moses had laid his hands on him. So the people of Israel obeyed him and did as the Lord had commanded Moses.
>
> Deuteronomy 34:9

Joshua's story is also incredibly inspiring, but like Moses's, it also begins in a place of doubt. And rightly so—after all, he is following Moses, someone he looked up to for years. But God, in His kindness, once again meets His people with faithfulness.

Three times in Joshua 1:5–9, God charges Joshua to be strong *and* courageous.

> Have I not commanded you? Be strong and courageous. Do not be frightened, and do not be dismayed, for the LORD your God is with you wherever you go.
>
> Joshua 1:9

In essence, God says:

1. Go be great.
2. Go be great.
3. Go be great!

That little third-grade girl of mine was on to something when she slammed the door and said, "GO BE GREAT."

I've got good news; the Israelites had a crazy journey, but they finally made it to the Promised Land.

And you, my friend, you will find your way too. Whether your transition season is leading you to a place of development, separation, cultivation, or to a place of being finished, the Lord your God is with you wherever you go.

I know you will still battle feelings of loneliness, fear, and worry. You may feel like you are in your own wilderness for years and years. But if you decide to keep growing with God in each season of your life, He will always lead you.

You have a purpose beyond anything you can see today. Trust the process. And . . .

GO BE GREAT.

End-of-Seasons
Mini Bible Study

Read Exodus 17:8–16

Who was the war against?

A. The Egyptians
B. The Amalekites
C. The Israelites

This is an incredible story we just didn't have the space to include in the chapters, so I wanted to include it here.

Who were the Amalekites?

The following is from the Expositor's Bible Commentary:

The Amalekites lived in the desert, south of Canaan around Kadesh (Genesis 14:7) otherwise known as the northern part of the Negev. . . . Amalek was the son of Eliphaz (Esau's oldest boy) . . . and became a "clan" or "chief" in the tribe of Esau. . . . the Amalekites were distant cousins to the Israelites.[1]

What was Moses's plan to defeat their attack? (Exodus 17:9)

What happened to Moses's arms in Exodus 17:11–12?

Who held his arms up?

Read Exodus 25 and write out as many details as you can about the tabernacle:

Write out John 1:14:

_____

_____

_____

This word for "dwelt" in Greek is *eskenosen*, which means he *pitched his tent* among us. It is quite plain that John is saying that he "*tabernacled* among us, and we have seen his glory," just as the glory of God filled the tabernacle in Exodus 40:35 and Solomon's temple in 1 Kings 8:11.

Read Deuteronomy 34

What is the name of the mountain Moses went up on?

_____

What do you think it was like for Moses to lay his eyes on the Promised Land, knowing he would not enter?

_____

_____

How old was Moses when he died?

   A. 100
   B. 130
   C. 120

What are your takeaways from studying the life of Moses?

Five Steps to Finish Well

When we are thinking about our own process of finishing well, sometimes we need a little guidance to help us. Below are five steps we can take to finish seasons well.

1. Failing to make plans is planning to fail.

One of the things that has helped me so much in the transitions of my life is to make plans weekly that give me something to look forward to. Sometimes it's something big, like a speaking engagement I get to turn into a little trip with a friend.

And other times it's something really simple, like meeting a friend for a walk at the park.

Create opportunities where there seems to be nothing. Dig deep. Get creative. And start making plans to help you love your life today.

But also, when you sense a season is finished, begin making the plans to end it well. Maybe you need to type out your resignation letter, start looking for a replacement, or do whatever you need to do to finish well.

2. Don't partner with thoughts that don't please God.

In seasons of transition, it can be easy to become addicted to discouragement. We start to expect it if we've been in a transition for too long. Today can be the day you wake up and make a decision to not partner YOUR thoughts with anything that doesn't please God. This includes thoughts like:

- Things were so much better back then (fill in your "back then").
- No one believes in me.
- There's nothing good coming in my life.

3. Read more.

First, kudos to you if you've made it this far in this book! You *are* reading. It's good to remind ourselves of the importance of doing certain things in order to keep growing. According to healthline .com, here are a few things that reading regularly can do:

- improves brain connectivity
- increases your vocabulary and comprehension
- empowers you to empathize with other people
- aids in sleep readiness
- reduces stress
- lowers blood pressure and heart rate
- fights depression symptoms
- prevents cognitive decline as you age

Circle the benefits you need the most right now.

There is much research coming out about our phones and computers and how unwell they can make our minds. But I've never read a research article that said reading had any negative effects. Unless you are reading straight-up horror fiction. Don't recommend that.

Keep your mind busy and full of new knowledge when a season is ending.

4. Give yourself daily compassion.

We are the hardest on ourselves. Remember the kindness that God showed the Israelites in the midst of their transition to the Promised Land? God is showing you kindness too.

What would it look like for you to begin to give yourself daily compassion and receive God's kindness in your life?

5. Don't look back more than you look ahead.

It is good to remember God's faithfulness in each season of our lives. But remember, we have to be careful not to look back on what is over and doubt there are good things ahead. You may need to look back on a season and recognize the lessons it taught you, the people that you may need to forgive, or the disappointments you experienced.

Notes

To the Reader

1. Bruce Feiler, *Life Is in the Transitions* (New York: Penguin, 2020), 72, 157.

Chapter 1 The Four Seasons

1. Dictionary.com, s.v. "development," https://www.dictionary.com/browse /development.

2. Dictionary.com, s.v. "separation," https://www.dictionary.com/browse /separation.

3. Dictionary.com, s.v. "cultivate," https://www.dictionary.com/browse /cultivate.

4. Dictionary.com, s.v. "finished," https://www.dictionary.com/browse /finished.

Chapter 2 Change for You

1. David Guzik, "Exodus 2—Moses' Birth and Early Career," Enduring Word, 2018, https://enduringword.com/bible-commentary/exodus-2/.

Chapter 8 The Fear of Not Knowing If It's God

1. "Sweet Brown on Apartment Fire," YouTube video, 0:41, posted by KFO R Oklahoma News on April 11, 2012, https://www.youtube.com/watch?v=ydm Ph4MXT3g.

End-of-Seasons Mini Bible Study

1. Frank E. Gaebelein, general editor, *The Expositor's Bible Commentary, vol. 2* (Grand Rapids, MI: Zondervan, 1990), 407–408.

Nicki Koziarz is a bestselling author and speaker with Proverbs 31 Ministries. She speaks nationally at conferences, retreats, and meetings, and hosts her own podcast, *Lessons from the Farm*. A Bible teacher at heart, Nicki inspires others to become the best version of who God created them to be through the Scriptures. Nicki, her husband, and their family run a small farm just outside of Charlotte, North Carolina, they affectionately call The Fixer Upper Farm. Learn more at nickikoziarz.com.

More from Nicki Koziarz

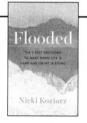
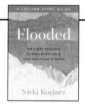
BETHANYHOUSE

Stay up to date on your favorite books and authors with our free e-newsletters. Sign up today at bethanyhouse.com.

 facebook.com/BHPnonfiction

 @bethany_house

 @bethany_house_nonfiction